Contents

Move Your Body

Concepts:

Muscles and bones work together to move the body.

Muscles contract and release.

Define It!

contract: to make something smaller or shorter; to tighten

release: to stop holding; to let go

tendon: a band of tissue that connects muscles to bones

tissue: the material that forms parts of the body

Have you ever thought about how your body moves? When you want to take a step, your brain sends a signal to your leg and tells it to move. But it's your muscles and bones that do the actual moving. Muscles and bones are types of **tissue** that work together. They support your body and allow it to move.

Muscles are attached to bones by small bands of tissue called **tendons**. When muscles

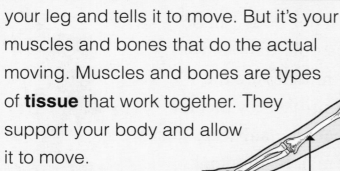

muscle tissue

bone tissue

contract and **release**, they cause the attached bones to move. When you "make a muscle" by bending your arm, you are actually contracting the muscle tissue, making it shorter and thicker. This causes your elbow to bend and raises your lower arm. When you stop bending, the muscle tissue releases, becoming longer and thinner.

What kind of tissue do you think each body part is mostly made of? Write *muscle tissue* or *bone tissue*.

1. your kneecaps   *bone tissue*

2. your tongue   *muscle tissue*

Muscles and Bones

Muscles and Bones

Muscles

The muscles in our body are made of soft tissue. Soft tissue connects, surrounds, and supports the other parts of the body. Types of soft tissue include muscles, tendons, fat, and skin.

All of the muscles in our body can be divided into two groups: **voluntary** and **involuntary**. Voluntary muscles are the muscles that you can control. They include your abdominals (stomach), quadriceps (thighs), and biceps (arms). Involuntary muscles work automatically. These muscles include your heart and the muscles that line your **intestines**. Your heart pumps without you having to tell it to. The muscles in your intestines push food down without you thinking about it.

Define It!

intestines: long tubes that help digest food after it has left the stomach

involuntary: done without thinking or being aware of

voluntary: controlled; on purpose

The biceps are voluntary muscles.

The heart is an involuntary muscle.

Write *true* or *false*.

1. Your heart is a voluntary muscle. ___*false*___
   involuntary

2. Muscles, tendons, and skin are soft tissues. ___*true*___

3. Your brain tells your biceps to contract. ___*false*___

Bones

The bones in our body are made of hard tissue. Hard tissue protects parts of the body and provides support. For example, the bones of your ribcage protect your lungs and heart. Your femur, or thighbone, provides support for the muscles in your upper leg. Bones and **cartilage** are two types of hard tissues in humans. Some animals have other types of hard tissue such as antlers or shells.

Our bones cannot move by themselves. They need muscles that contract and release to put them in motion. But muscles can't contract and release without being attached to something hard and **rigid**, like bones. In order for our bodies to move, we need both muscles and bones.

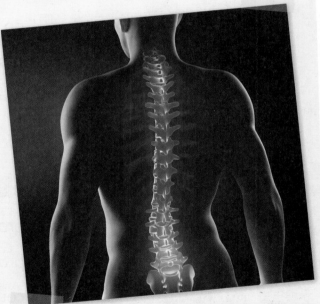

The spine provides support for the head, neck, and trunk.

Muscles and Bones

Why do we need both muscles and bones to move our body?

We do need both our muscles and bones because the muscles can't contract and release without being attached to something hard and rigid like bones. In order for our bodies to move.

Function and Form

Look at the pictures of different muscles and bones in the body. Then mark an **X** in the box of the correct answer for each question.

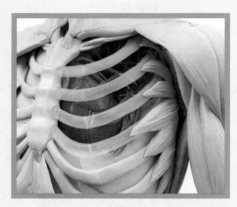

bones: ribcage
muscle: heart

1. What does the ribcage do?

☐ provides support for the heart

☑ protects the heart

☐ helps the heart move

2. What type of muscle is the heart?

☑ an involuntary muscle

☐ a bending muscle

☐ a voluntary muscle

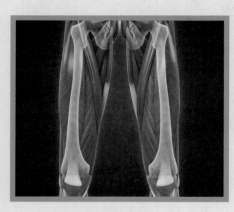

bone: femur
muscles: quadriceps

1. What does the femur do?

☑ provides support for the quadriceps

☐ protects the quadriceps

☐ contracts the quadriceps muscle

2. What type of muscles are the quadriceps?

☐ involuntary muscles

☐ rigid muscles

☑ voluntary muscles

Muscles and Bones

Either/Or Questions

Write each answer.

1. Is a contracted muscle shorter and thicker **or** longer and thinner?

   thicker, shorter

2. Does your brain tell voluntary muscles to move **or** do they move automatically?

   your brain has to tell

3. Is muscle tissue hard **or** soft?   _soft_

4. Do tendons connect bones to other bones, muscles to other muscles, **or** muscles to bones?

   muscles to bones

5. Is hard tissue bendable **or** is it rigid?   _rigid_

6. Is the heart **or** the biceps an involuntary muscle? _heart_

7. When you release a muscle, are you tightening it **or** letting it go?

   letting it go

8. Is cartilage considered a hard tissue **or** a soft tissue?

   soft tissus

Muscles and Bones

Muscles Work in Pairs

When you bend your arm to make a muscle, your biceps contracts. But did you know that another muscle, your triceps, releases at the same time? Muscles work in pairs to move bones. One contracts while the other releases. In this activity, you will make a model arm to show how the biceps and triceps muscles work together.

What You Need

- table tennis ball or other ball
- 2 cardboard toilet paper tubes
- 2 long rubber bands
- 2 large paper clips
- pushpin
- masking tape
- glue
- ruler

Directions

1. Measure 1.2 inches (3 cm) down from one end of Tube 1. Using the pushpin, poke a hole on each side of the tube.

2. Straighten a paper clip. Push the clip through the holes in Tube 1. Bend the ends of the paper clip up toward the open end of the tube.

3. Loop a rubber band around each of the bent ends of the paper clip. Wrap masking tape around the tube to cover the ends of the clip.

4. Glue the ball to Tube 2 as shown.

5. Repeat Steps 1 and 2 for Tube 2 on the end opposite the ball.

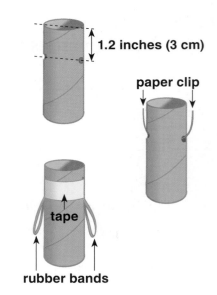

1.2 inches (3 cm)

paper clip

tape

rubber bands

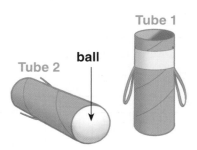

Tube 1

Tube 2

ball

Muscles and Bones

8

6. Place Tube 1 and Tube 2 together as shown. Then stretch the rubber bands of Tube 1 down to the bent ends of the paper clip of Tube 2 and loop them around. Wrap masking tape around Tube 2 to cover the bent ends of the clip.

7. Tape one rubber band to the cardboard tube "lower arm" as shown. Tape the other rubber band to the back of the ball as shown.

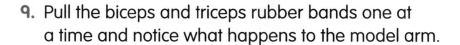

8. Bend and straighten the model arm and notice what happens to the rubber bands.

9. Pull the biceps and triceps rubber bands one at a time and notice what happens to the model arm.

What Did You Discover?

1. What happened to the biceps rubber band when you bent the arm? What happened to the triceps rubber band?

   _____

   _____

2. What happened when you pulled on the biceps rubber band?

   _____

3. What happened when you pulled on the triceps rubber band?

   _____

4. How does this activity show that muscles work in pairs to move bones?

   _____

   _____

   _____

Muscles and Bones

Muscles and Bones

Move It or Lose It

Simple exercises can help you think about how muscles are responsible for movement. Perform each exercise below, and then write down which muscles you think you were using. Use the diagram to help you name the muscles.

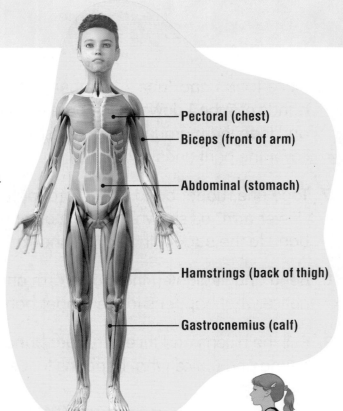

- Pectoral (chest)
- Biceps (front of arm)
- Abdominal (stomach)
- Hamstrings (back of thigh)
- Gastrocnemius (calf)

1. Toe Raises

Stand with feet flat on the floor, holding a table or chair for support. Rise up on your toes as high as you can. Lower yourself slowly.

_____

2. Crunches

Lie on your back with your knees bent and your feet flat on the floor. Place your hands behind your neck for support. Keeping your lower back on the floor, gently raise your head and shoulders off the floor. Lower your head and shoulders.

_____

3. Leg Curls

Lie facedown with your legs straight. Bend your knees and bring your heels toward your backside. Straighten your legs again.

_____

Concepts:

Skin is an organ that protects the body.

Skin is made up of epithelial and connective tissue.

Tissues of the Skin

Define It!

connective tissue: tissue that provides structure and support to the body

epithelial tissue: tissue that covers the inside and outside surfaces of the body

organ: a group of tissues that perform specific functions

temperature: a measure of the heat of a person's body

You may not think of your skin as an **organ**, but it is. In fact, it is the largest organ of your body. Your skin keeps your body from drying out. It also helps to keep your **temperature** constant and blocks disease.

Skin is made up of two types of tissue: **epithelial tissue** and **connective tissue**. Connective tissue supports and connects other tissues in the body. But when you look at your skin, you are seeing epithelial tissue. Epithelial tissue protects the body from the outside world. It keeps the body from losing fluids. It also releases sweat, which keeps us cool.

Name three things that epithelial tissue does.

1. It releases sweat, which keeps us cool.
2. Epithelial tissue protects the body from the outside world!
3. connetcive tissue supports + connects other tissue in the body.

Skin

Concept:

There are three layers of skin: the hypodermis, dermis, and epidermis.

Layers of the Skin

Define It!

dermis: the middle layer of skin

epidermis: the outer layer of skin

hypodermis: the bottom layer of skin

There are three layers of skin. The bottom layer is called the **hypodermis**. The hypodermis is a layer of fat and connective tissue that helps connect the skin to muscles and bones.

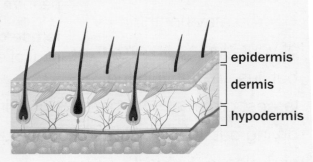

The middle layer of skin, the **dermis**, is made mostly of connective tissue. The dermis includes hair roots, nerve endings, and sweat glands. The dermis cushions the body and controls body heat. It also allows us to feel pain, temperature, and pressure.

The top layer of skin is called the **epidermis**. The epidermis is made of epithelial tissue. It protects the other layers of your skin and prevents your body from losing water.

Answer the questions.

1. Which layer of skin is the bottom layer?   *hypdermis*

2. Which layer protects the other layers of skin?   *epidermis*

3. Which layer contains hair roots?   *dermis*

Callus and Sebum

Define It!

callus: a dry, tough layer of skin

friction: the rubbing of one object against another

sebum: an oily substance that covers the epidermis

Concepts:

A callus is tough, thick tissue that keeps the skin from getting damaged.

Sebum is an oily substance that keeps your skin from absorbing too much water.

The epidermis layer of skin helps to protect the body. But what protects the epidermis? Sometimes, layers of tough and dry tissue form on the epidermis to keep the skin from getting damaged. When there is a lot of **friction** on your skin, the layers of tissue build up to become thick and hard. This is what we call a **callus**. Calluses most often develop on the feet and hands.

An oily substance called **sebum** also protects your skin. Sebum acts like a natural waterproof seal. It keeps your skin from absorbing too much water. Sebum also helps keep water inside the skin so it doesn't dry out.

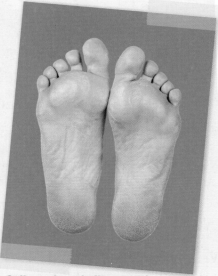

Calluses have built up on the heels and balls of the feet.

Why do you think calluses most often develop on the feet and hands?

orally

_____

_____

_____

Skin

The Three Layers

Look at the diagram of the three layers of skin. Label the *dermis*, *epidermis*, and *hypodermis*.

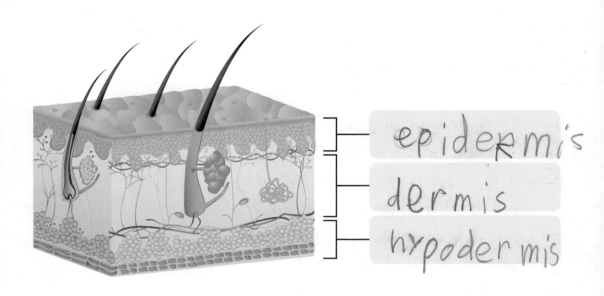

epidermis

dermis

hypodermis

Write which layer of skin—the *hypodermis*, *dermis*, or *epidermis*—is described in each statement below.

1. calluses and sebum are found here   eperdermis

2. is responsible for sense of touch   dermis

3. prevents your body from losing water   epidermis

4. is a layer of fat and connective tissue   hypodermis

5. helps you feel pressure and temperature   n dermis

6. connects skin to muscles and bones   chypodermis
                                             tissue

7. includes nerve endings   dermis

Our Bodies and Our Senses   Skill Sharpeners—Science • EMC 5324 • © Evan-Moor Corp.

Skin Crossword Puzzle

Skill:

Apply content vocabulary.

Use the vocabulary words to complete the crossword puzzle.

| dermis | callus | connective | epidermis |
| sebum | epithelial | organ | friction |

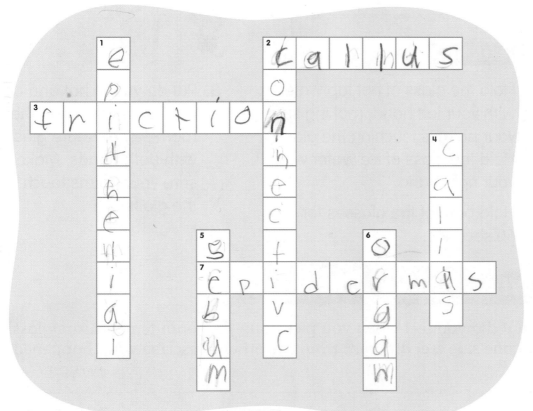

Across

2. a dry, tough layer of skin

3. the rubbing of one object against another

7. the outer layer of skin

Down

1. a type of tissue that covers the inside and outside surfaces of the body

2. a type of tissue that provides structure and support to the body

4. the middle layer of skin

5. an oily substance that covers the epidermis

6. a group of tissues that perform specific functions

What Do You Feel?

In this experiment, you will test your skin's ability to feel differences in temperature.

What You Need

- 3 tall glasses of water: 1 with hot tap water, 1 with room-temperature water, 1 with ice water

- stopwatch to time yourself

Directions

1. Hold the glass of hot tap water with your left hand, making sure your palm is touching the glass. Hold the glass of ice water with your right hand.

2. Hold both of the glasses for 60 seconds.

3. Put down the hot and cold glasses and pick up the room-temperature glass with both hands. Make sure your palms touch the glass.

What Did You Discover?

What did you feel when you picked up the room-temperature glass? Did one side feel different from the other? Describe what happened.

_____

_____

_____

_____

What Happened?

Your skin does not feel the exact temperature of an object. Instead, your skin can sense the difference in temperature of a new object compared to the temperature of the object it last touched.

skin

Sense of Touch

Is your skin equally sensitive all over your body? Try this experiment to find out.

Skills:
Conduct experiments and draw conclusions about the results.

What You Need

- ruler
- 2 toothpicks
- a partner

Directions

1. Explain to your partner that you will lightly touch him/her with either one or two toothpicks. Make sure your partner keeps his/her eyes closed.

2. Without telling your partner, hold two toothpicks so that the points measure .25 inch (.6 cm) apart and touch him/her on the fingertip. Ask your partner if he/she felt one or two points. If he/she says one, separate the two toothpicks so that they are .5 inch (1.3 cm) apart and touch him/her again.

3. Repeat this exercise by moving the toothpicks farther and farther apart until your partner feels two points. Mark an **X** on the chart at the measurement where he/she felt two points.

4. Repeat Steps 2 and 3 with the other body parts given on the chart.

	.25 in. (.6 cm)	.5 in. (1.3 cm)	.75 in. (2 cm)	1 in. (2.5 cm)
Fingertip				
Upper Arm				
Back				

What Did You Discover?

1. Which part of your partner's body was most sensitive? Explain why.

_____

_____

2. Which part of your partner's body was least sensitive? Explain why.

_____

_____

Skin

Protect Your Skin

Name some of the ways that your skin protects your body. Then write about the ways that your body protects your skin. Include information about what happens in the different layers of the skin.

_____

_____

_____

_____

_____

_____

_____

Make Connections

What are some things you do to protect and take care of your skin?

_____

_____

_____

Skin

Concepts:

The eyes take in light and send signals to the brain, which tells us what we are looking at.

The parts of the eye we can see are the sclera, iris, and pupil.

Parts of the Eye

Define It!

iris: the colored part of the eye that controls the amount of light that can enter

pupil: the dark circle in the center of the iris where light enters the eye

sclera: the white part of the eye that controls movement

spherical: shaped like a ball or globe

Have you ever wondered how you are able to see? Our eyes are the organs that control our sense of sight. They take in light and send signals to the brain. The brain then tells us what we are seeing.

Even though eyes may appear circular or almond-shaped, they are really **spherical**. The parts of the eye that we can see are the **sclera**, **iris**, and **pupil**. The sclera is the white part of the eye. It contains muscles that control the eye's movement. The iris is the colored part of the eye. It controls the amount of light that can enter the eye. The pupil is the dark circle in the center of the iris. Light enters the eye through the pupil.

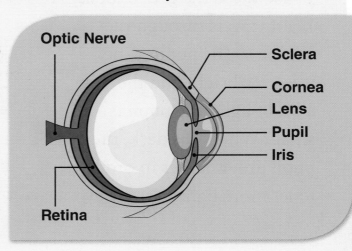

Optic Nerve — Sclera — Cornea — Lens — Pupil — Iris — Retina

Eyesight

Answer the questions.

1. What shape are our eyes? ___spherical___

2. Which part of the eye controls its movement? ___sclera___

Concepts:

Light reflects off objects and travels in a straight line into the eye.

Light enters the eye through the cornea to the pupil.

Eyesight

Light Enters the Eye

To see the world around you, your eyes need light. Eyes send your brain information about an object's shape, color, and movement. They do this by taking in light that **reflects** off that object. Light reflected off an object travels in a straight line into the eye.

Light enters the eye through the **cornea**. The cornea is a clear coating that covers the iris and pupil at the front of the eye. It helps to **refract**, or change the direction of the light. It also helps the eye to focus. Light travels through the cornea to the pupil. When it is very bright and there is a lot of light, the pupil is small. When it is dark, the pupil grows larger in order to let more light into the eye.

Write *true* or *false*.

1. Light travels in a straight line into the eye. _true_

2. The pupil grows larger when it is bright out. _false_

3. The cornea helps to refract light. _true_

How We See

After light passes through your pupil, it travels to the **lens**. The lens helps to focus the light to a part on the back of the eye called the **retina**. Because the lens refracts light, the image **projected** to the retina is upside down! The retina's job is to change the projected image into nerve signals. These signals are sent through the **optic nerve** to the brain. The brain is then able to make sense of what you are seeing.

Say you are looking at a tree. In an instant, you are able to tell that it is a tree because light reflected off the tree and traveled in a straight line into your pupil. The lens refracted the light and projected the image to your retina. The retina changed the image into nerve signals, which traveled along the optic nerve to your brain. Then your brain told you, "It's a tree!"

Define It!

lens: the part of the eye that focuses and refracts light

optic nerve: nerves that send signals from the eye to the brain

project: to cause light to appear on a surface

retina: a layer at the back of the eye that changes images into nerve signals

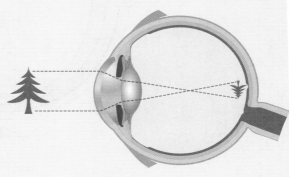

Concepts:

The lens refracts light to the retina.

The retina changes images into nerve signals that travel through the optic nerve to the brain.

Eyesight

Complete the sentences.

1. The _____optic nerve_____ sends signals to the brain.

2. The lens projects an image onto the _____retina_____.

Skills:

Interpret and identify information in graphic representations.

The Eyes Have It

Look at the numbered diagram of the eye. Next to each matching number and description below, label the *cornea, iris, lens, optic nerve, pupil, retina,* and *sclera.*

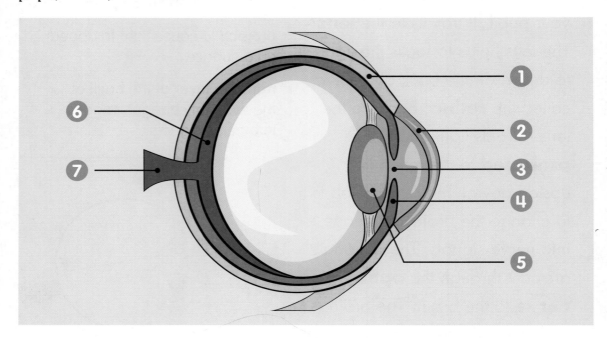

1. moves the eye — *sclera*

2. refracts light and helps the eye focus — *connea*

3. takes in light — *pupil*

4. controls the amount of light that enters the eye — *iris*

5. refracts light and focuses it to the back of the eye — *lensa*

6. transforms images into nerve signals — *retinaerve*

7. sends nerve signals to the brain — *optic nerve*

Skill:
Apply content vocabulary.

Either/Or Questions

Write each answer.

1. Is the pupil **or** the iris the colored part of the eye? _iris_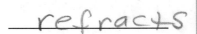

2. Does the lens take in **or** refract light? _refracts_

3. Is the sclera the white part **or** the colored part of the eye?
   white part

4. Is the eye circular **or** spherical in shape? Spherical

5. Is an image projected **or** reflected onto the retina?
   projected

6. Does the cornea **or** the optic nerve send signals to the brain?
   optic nerve

Eyesight

Skills:

Conduct experiments and draw conclusions about the results.

Blind Spot

Have you ever heard adults complain about a "blind spot" while driving? Perhaps they didn't see an oncoming car while they were changing lanes. We all have blind spots. Complete the activities to see (or rather, *not* see!) your blind spot in action.

What You Need

- 3" x 5" (8 cm x 13 cm) index card (or other stiff paper)

- pen or marker

- ruler

Directions

1. Mark a dot and an **X** on the card as shown.

2. Hold the card at eye level and about an arm's length away. Make sure that the **X** is on the right side.

3. Close your right eye and look directly at the **X** with your left eye. Notice that you can also see the dot. Focus on the **X** but be aware of the dot as you slowly bring the card closer to your face.

4. Now close your left eye and look directly at the dot with your right eye. As you slowly bring the card closer to your face, notice what happens to the **X**.

5. Repeat Steps 2–4, but this time hold the card so that it is at an angle.

Eyesight

6. Using the ruler, draw a straight line through the center of the dot and the **X** to both edges of the card.

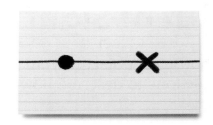

7. Repeat Step 3. Notice what happens to the dot and the line.

What Did You Discover?

1. What happened to the dot in Step 3?

   _____

2. What happened to the **X** in Step 4?

   _____

3. Were the results the same in Step 5? If not, explain your answer.

   _____

4. What happened to the dot and the line in Step 7?

   _____

What Happened?

The optic nerve passes through one spot on the retina. In this spot, the retina cannot receive light. When you hold the card so that the light from the dot or **X** falls on this spot, you cannot see the dot or the **X**. However, the line does not disappear, because your brain automatically "fills in" the blind spot. It does this by using information from the line that continued to the edges of the card.

Eyesight

Out of Sight

Choose an object in your room and focus on it. Now answer the questions to describe how you are able to see this object.

1. What is the object? _____

2. How does light enter your eye from the object?

   _____

   _____

3. Through which two parts of the eye does light enter?

   _____

4. Which part of the eye refracts the light onto the retina?

   _____

5. How does the image of your object appear on your retina?

   _____

6. What is the retina's job?

   _____

7. Which part of the eye sends nerve signals to the brain?

   _____

8. What happens when nerve signals reach your brain?

   _____

What Is Sound?

Concepts:

Objects make sound by vibrating to produce sound waves.

The faster an object vibrates, the higher the pitch of the sound.

Define It!

pitch: the highness or lowness of a sound

sound waves: waves of energy created when an object vibrates

vibrate: to move back and forth quickly

Your ears are amazing organs. They pick up all the sounds around you and tell your brain what you are hearing. They also help you keep your balance! But to understand how your ears work, you first need to understand what sound is.

Objects make sounds by **vibrating**, or moving quickly back and forth. These vibrations produce **sound waves** that move just like ripples in water. The highness or lowness of a sound is called the **pitch**. The faster an object vibrates, the higher the pitch of the sound. The slower an object vibrates, the lower the pitch of the sound. People can hear a wide range of sounds—from a low, deep drum to a high-pitched whistle and from a quiet whisper to loud rock music.

Hearing

Write the missing words.

1. The highness or lowness of a sound is called its _pitch_.

2. Objects make _Sound waves_ by vibrating.

Concept:

The pinna collects sound waves and helps to determine the direction of sound.

Hearing

Outer Ear

Define It!

ear canal: a long tube that runs from the outer ear to the middle ear

earwax: the waxy matter produced in the ear canal

pinna: the part of the ear you can see

The ear is made up of three different sections: the outer ear, middle ear, and inner ear. The **pinna** is the part of the outer ear that you can see. The main job of the pinna is to collect sound waves. The shape and position of the pinna helps you to determine the direction of a sound. If a sound is coming from

The pinna is the part of the ear you can see.

behind you or above you, it will bounce off the pinna in a different way than if it is coming from in front of you or below you. Because the pinna faces forward, you can hear sounds better in front of you than you can behind you.

The outer ear also includes the **ear canal**. This is where **earwax** is produced. Earwax fights germs that could hurt the skin inside the ear canal. Earwax also collects dirt to help keep the ear canal clean.

Answer the questions.

1. What is the main job of the pinna? _to colect sound_

2. Where is earwax produced? _in ear canal._

Middle and Inner Ear

Define It!

cochlea: a curved part of the inner ear that turns vibrations into signals

eardrum: a thin skin in the middle ear that vibrates when sound waves move through it

interpret: to make sense of

After sound waves enter the outer ear, they travel through the ear canal into the middle ear. The middle ear's main job is to turn those sound waves into vibrations and send them to the inner ear. To do this, the middle ear needs the **eardrum**, which is a thin piece of tightly stretched skin.

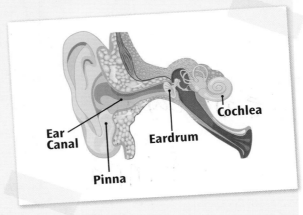

The eardrum separates the outer ear from tiny bones in the middle ear. When sound waves pass through the eardrum, they vibrate the bones in the middle ear before entering the inner ear.

The vibrations enter the inner ear through the **cochlea**. The job of the cochlea is to change sound vibrations into signals the brain can understand. The cochlea is filled with liquid, which ripples like a wave when the bones of the middle ear vibrate. These "waves" send out signals that the brain **interprets** as sound.

Write *true* or *false*.

1. The cochlea changes vibrations into signals. _true_

2. The eardrum is located in the inner ear. _middle_

Skill:

Label images that represent scientific concepts.

Parts of the Ear

Look at the diagram of the ear. Label the *cochlea, ear canal, eardrum,* and *pinna*.

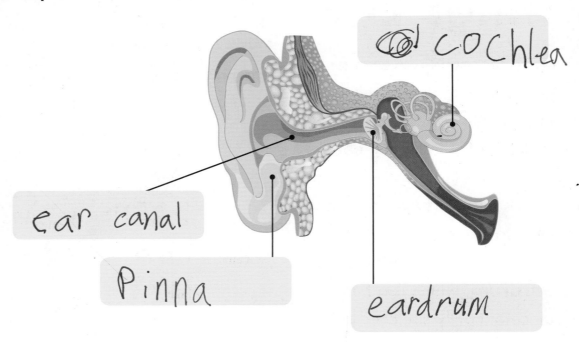

cochlea

ear canal

Pinna

eardrum

Fill in the blanks to describe the path that sound waves take through the ear.

Sound waves enter the ear through the _outer ear_.

They travel through the ear canal to the _eardrum_.

Sound waves vibrate tiny _bones_ in the

middle ear before entering the inner ear through the

cochlea. The cochlea changes the sound

vibrations into _signals_ the brain then

interpret as sound.

Hearing

Our Bodies and Our Senses   Skill Sharpeners—Science • EMC 5324 • © Evan-Moor Corp.

Hearing Crossword Puzzle

Use the vocabulary words to complete the crossword puzzle.

| cochlea | sound waves | vibrate | pinna |
| eardrum | interpret | pitch | ear canal |

Across

3. the part of the ear you can see
5. to move back and forth quickly
6. a part of the inner ear that changes sound vibrations into signals
7. a membrane in the middle ear that vibrates in response to sound waves
8. the highness or lowness of sound

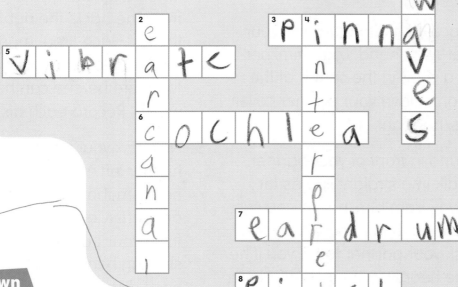

Down

1. waves of energy created when an object vibrates
2. a long tube that runs from the outer ear to the middle ear
4. to make sense of

Can You Hear Me Now?

Just how true is your sense of hearing? In this activity, you and a partner will listen closely for the ticking of a clock. You'll try to find out which ear hears better and which angles are best for hearing.

What You Need

- a partner
- watch or stopwatch that ticks
- cloth or towel to be used as a blindfold

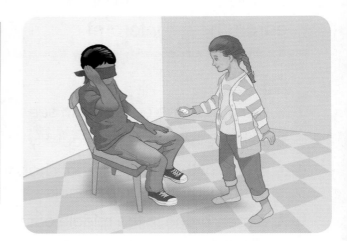

Directions

1. Find a large room that is not noisy.

2. Place a blindfold around your partner's head. Lead him/her to a chair in the center of the room. Have your partner cover his/her right ear.

3. Stand in front of your partner. Walk in a straight line as far away from him/her as you can. Hold up the ticking watch and ask your partner to tell you if he/she hears anything. Walk closer and closer until your partner says he/she can hear the watch. Measure the distance from your partner to where he/she can hear the watch. Record it in the chart on page 33.

4. Repeat Step 3 three more times. Approach your partner from the back, the right, and the left. Each time, measure the distance from your partner to where he/she can hear the watch. Record each distance.

5. Now ask your partner to cover his/her left ear. Approach him/her from the front, back, right, and left. Measure the distances from your partner to where he/she can hear the watch. Record each distance.

6. Have your partner uncover both ears and repeat the experiment.

Hearing

Skill Sharpeners—Science • EMC 5324 • © Evan-Moor Corp.

	Front distance	Back distance	Right side distance	Left side distance
Right ear covered				
Left ear covered				
Both ears uncovered				

What Did You Discover?

1. Which ear—right or left—could hear the ticking watch from the farthest distance? What was the distance? Where did the sound come from: the front, back, right side, or left side?

_____

_____

_____

2. At which angles was it easier to hear the ticking watch? Which angles made it more difficult to hear?

_____

_____

_____

3. How did hearing with both ears compare to hearing with one ear?

_____

_____

_____

Hearing

Skill:

Write narratives to develop real or imagined experiences or events.

Catch a Sound Wave

Pretend that you are a high-pitched sound wave. Describe your journey through the ear and how you think the person acted when he or she heard your sound.

Choose one of these sounds, or use your own idea:

- **a whistle**
- **tires screeching**
- **an opera singer's voice**

Hint

An object makes sound waves when it vibrates. The faster it vibrates, the higher the pitch of the sound.

_____

_____

_____

_____

_____

_____

Concept:
Weathering and erosion help to shape our planet's surface.

Shaping Our Planet's Surface

Define It!

erosion: the moving of rocks and soil by water, wind, ice, or gravity

gravity: a force that pulls objects toward the center of Earth

landform: a natural feature of Earth's surface

weathering: the breaking down or wearing away of rocks by water or wind

Earth's surface is made up of many **landforms**. These landforms include mountains, valleys, islands, and canyons. The landforms on Earth have been shaped and reshaped by natural forces. Two of the most important forces in shaping our planet's surface are **weathering** and **erosion**.

Weathering is the breaking down or wearing away of rocks by water or wind. Have you ever picked up a very smooth rock on the beach? The smoothness of the rock is a result of the weathering waves of the ocean and the wind blowing on the beach. Erosion is the moving of rocks and soil by water, wind, ice, or **gravity**. High waves on a beach can erode sand dunes, carrying the sand back into the ocean.

Weathering & Erosion

Name one example of weathering and one example of erosion from the text.

1. weathering: _the breaking down_

2. erosion: _the moving of rock and soil by water, wind, ice, or gravity_

Layers of Rock

Define It!

deposit: to put or set something down in a specific place

sediment: very small pieces of sand and minerals set down by water, wind, or ice

spectacular: beautiful in an eye-catching way

One of Earth's most **spectacular** natural features is the mile-deep Grand Canyon in northern Arizona. It is also one of the best examples of weathering and erosion. Visitors can look from the rim of the canyon to see the Colorado River far below. The walls of the canyon have many layers of different kinds of rock. Some of the rocks are as much as two billion years old!

Over millions of years, small pieces of sand called **sediment** were **deposited** in the area where the Grand Canyon formed. As new layers of sediment were deposited, the older layers were pressed down. Over time, they became solid layers of rock. But it wasn't until five or six million years ago that weathering and erosion began cutting into the rock to form the canyon.

Answer the questions.

1. How deep is the Grand Canyon?

   mile deep

2. About when did the Grand Canyon begin to form?

Shaping the Grand Canyon

Concept:

Erosion and weathering helped to form the Grand Canyon.

Five or six million years ago, the Grand Canyon began to take shape. When rain fell, water ran down the **sloping** land of the Rocky Mountains. This eroded the soil, making **channels**. Over time, the channels became the path for the Colorado River. Over millions of years, the Colorado River kept eroding the soil and carving out the canyon.

Weathering also helped form the canyon. Rainwater ran into cracks in the rocks and froze in the winter. When the water froze, it **expanded** and pushed the rocks apart. Gravity caused sections of the canyon wall to fall, making the canyon wider. Wind also shaped the canyon. Bits of sand, blown by wind, chipped away at the canyon walls and weathered the rock. All these forces are at work even today, and they continue to change the canyon.

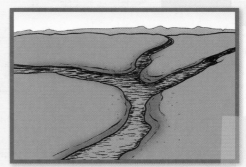
5 million years ago

Today

Weathering & Erosion

Circle all of the things that helped to shape the Grand Canyon.

gravity	earthquakes	wind
rainwater	mudslides	ice

Skills:

Interpret
and identify
information in
photographs.

Weathered Rock

Look at the pictures of the rocks. On the lines below, describe what each rock looks like. Write down their colors, textures, and shapes. Then tell which one you think has been more weathered and why.

_____   _____

_____   _____

_____   _____

_____   _____

Which rock looks more weathered? Why?

_____

_____

_____

Weathering/Erosion Crossword Puzzle

Use the vocabulary words to complete the crossword puzzle.

| ~~spectacular~~ | landform | channels | ~~sloping~~ |
| ~~weathering~~ | sediment | ~~erosion~~ | ~~expand~~ |

Across

3. a natural feature of Earth's surface

4. cuts in the ground made by moving water

8. the moving of rocks and soil by water, wind, ice, or gravity

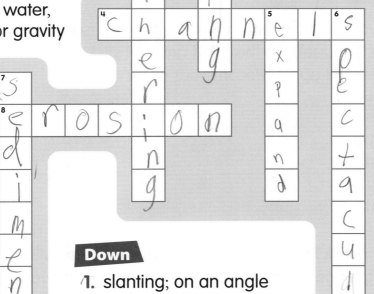

Down

1. slanting; on an angle

2. the breaking down or wearing away of rocks by water or wind

5. to become larger

6. beautiful in an eye-catching way

7. very small pieces of sand and minerals set down by water, wind, or ice

Weathering & Erosion

Hands-on Activity

Skills:

Conduct experiments and draw conclusions about the results.

Weathering & Erosion

Home Erosion

Have you ever made a sand castle on the beach? Chances are, it wasn't very long before the castle was knocked down. What might make your sand castle stronger? And how does erosion affect sand castles or other structures made of sand and soil? Find out in this experiment.

What You Need

- sand
- soil
- 2 buckets
- 4 plastic cups
- portable fan (with batteries)
- garden hose with sprayer

Directions

1. Before you start the experiment, look at the sand and soil. How do they feel? Do the sand and soil stick together easily, or do they fall apart? Record your observations.

Chart 1	Description
Sand, before experiment	
Soil, before experiment	

2. Make a prediction. Which structure do you think will stay standing longer—one made of dry sand or one made of dry soil? Explain your answer.

_____

_____

3. Pack one plastic cup with dry sand and turn it upside down on the ground in order to make a structure. Repeat the same thing with another plastic cup and the dry soil.

4. Create mud by mixing some of the soil with water in one bucket. In the other bucket, create wet sand by mixing some of the sand with just enough water to make it stick together.

5. Now make two more structures, one with mud and one with wet sand.

6. Blow on each of the structures one at a time, using the fan. Record what you observe in Chart 2.

7. Reusing the plastic cups, make four more structures by repeating Steps 3, 4, and 5.

8. Holding the hose, stand about 2 feet from your structures. Spray all the structures for about 30 seconds and then turn off the sprayer. Record what you observe in Chart 2.

Chart 2	Dry Soil	Dry Sand	Mud	Wet Sand
Wind (fan)				
Water (hose)				

What Did You Discover?

1. Which structure fell down first to the fan? Which stood up the best?

_____

_____

2. Which structure stood up best against the water?

_____

Weathering & Erosion

Skills:

Write an opinion piece supporting a point of view with reasons.

Draw illustrations that show scientific concepts.

Weathering & Erosion

How the Canyon Became Grand

Think about how the land in the area of the Grand Canyon probably looked five million years ago. Think about how it looks now. In what ways has it changed? Explain what forces helped to make those changes.

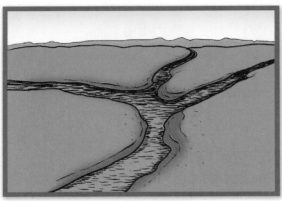
5 million years ago

Today

_____

_____

_____

_____

_____

What do you think the Grand Canyon will look like five million years in the future? Draw it.

Draw It!

Concept:
Glaciers are large sheets of ice that are found in places that are cold year-round.

What Are Glaciers?

Define It!

glacier: a slow-moving mass of ice

pressure: the weight or force produced when something presses against something else

Have you ever seen a snow-topped mountain? If so, you may have been looking at a **glacier**. Glaciers are large sheets of ice that form in places where more snow falls than melts. As layers of snow build upon one another, the weight from the top layers presses down on the layers underneath. This **pressure** turns the snow to ice, like when you squeeze fluffy snow into a hard snowball.

Because glaciers form slowly, most are found in places that are cold year-round. These places include Greenland, Antarctica, Alaska, and the tops of mountains.

This glacier sits on top of a mountain in Chile.

Complete the sentences.

1. Glaciers can only be found in places that are _____ throughout the entire year.

2. Glaciers form in places where more _____ falls than melts.

Moving Ice

Glaciers might appear to stay in one place, but they are actually "rivers" of ice that flow downhill. Glaciers can **advance** and **retreat** great distances, depending on the amount of snow that has fallen or ice that has melted. When a glacier advances, it flows farther downhill or spreads out. When a glacier retreats, it moves backward. This is because the ice is melting faster than the glacier is growing.

Glaciers are the largest moving objects on Earth, scraping rocks and soil from their paths like giant bulldozers. Movement of these **massive** sheets of ice can reshape the land over thousands of years.

Look at the diagram of a glacier. The lines show how far the ice retreated between the years 1850 and 2000.

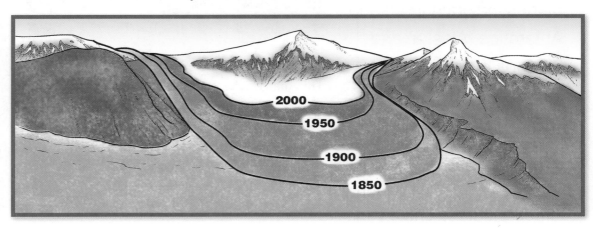

During which period of time did the glacier retreat the most?

1900 – 1950

orally

Glaciers Shape the Land

Concepts:

Glaciers shape the land by erosion.

Glaciers can leave behind moraines and basins.

One way that glaciers shape the surface of our planet is by erosion. The ice carries broken rocks and soil over long distances and deposits the **debris** far from its original location. One of the best examples of this kind of erosion is California's Yosemite Valley. Huge glaciers carved a giant U-shaped valley in the rock and left behind **ridges** of dirt and gravel called **moraines**.

In other places, erosion by glaciers created lakes. The Great Lakes were formed from **basins** scooped out by moving glaciers. When the ice melted, these basins filled with water.

Yosemite Valley

Glaciers

Name two famous places created by glaciers.

1. Yosemite

2. GL

Moraines and Basins

Look at the diagram. Label the *glacier*, *moraines*, and *basin*.

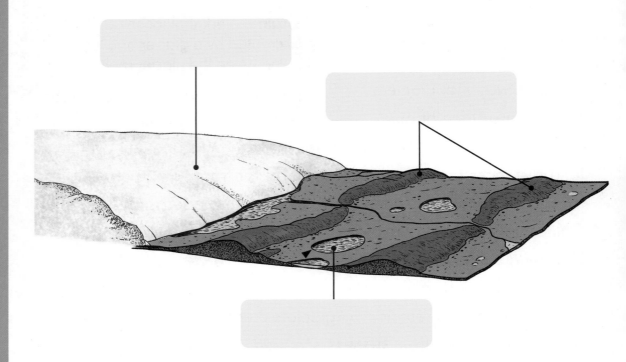

Write *true* or *false*.

1. Moraines create ridges of loose rock and soil. _true_

2. Moving glaciers can scoop out basins in the land. _true_

3. When glaciers melt, they can leave behind moraines.
   true

4. Both basins and moraines are created by erosion from glaciers.
   false

5. The Great Lakes were formed from moraines created by glaciers.
   false

Either/Or Questions

Write each answer.

1. Is something that is massive very large **or** very small? ✓

   _____large e_____

2. When a glacier moves backward, is it advancing **or** retreating? ✓

   _____

3. Were the Great Lakes formed from basins **or** moraines? ✓

   _____

4. Does pressure from the weight of the snow **or** erosion of the land help to form glaciers?

   _____

5. Is debris deposited by mountains **or** by glaciers?

   _____

6. When a glacier flows farther downhill, is it retreating **or** advancing?

   _____

7. Are moraines large holes in the ground **or** ridges of dirt and gravel?

   _____

Grinding Glaciers

In this activity, you will look at the effect that the movement of glaciers has on Earth's surface. You will use "sandy" ice cubes as a model of a glacier that has pieces of rock in its ice.

What You Need

- ice cube tray
- water
- several handfuls of clean sand
- aluminum foil
- plastic tub
- paper to cover the table
- paper towels for cleanup

Directions

1. Make "sandy" ice cubes by sprinkling sand into an ice cube tray filled with water and freezing it overnight.

2. Smooth out a sheet of foil on the top of a table or desk.

3. Rub an ice cube across the sheet of foil. Record what you observe in the chart on page 49.

4. Stack all the ice cubes inside one corner of the plastic tub and allow them to melt. Record what you observe.

Glaciers

	Observations
Ice cube on foil	
Ice cubes in tub	

What Did You Discover?

1. What happened when you rubbed the ice cube across the foil?

_____

2. What was left in the plastic tub after the ice cubes melted? What would this be called when a real glacier melts?

_____

3. What did the experiment show you about the ways that glaciers change Earth's surface?

_____

_____

Skill:

Write an opinion piece supporting a point of view with reasons.

Melting Ice

Today we live in a very warm period, and glaciers are on the move—backward! Most glaciers are melting faster than they are growing, and this has scientists worried about the future of our planet.

This sign reads "The glacier was here in 1908."

Pretend that you are a scientist studying the impact of the changing glaciers on the world today. What are five questions you would ask?

Example

What might happen if all the glaciers in Antarctica were to completely melt?

1. _____

2. _____

3. _____

4. _____

5. _____

A Surface Made of Plates

Define It!

fault: a break in Earth's crust where blocks of rock are moving in different directions

gradual: taking place slowly

mantle: a layer of molten rock beneath Earth's crust

plates: large sections of Earth's crust

Concepts:

Earth's crust is made up of plates.

When the plates move suddenly, an earthquake happens.

The outer layer of Earth is called the crust. The crust is made of different kinds of rock. Earth's crust is broken into many large pieces called **plates**. All the land and oceans on Earth lie on top of these plates. Beneath the plates is the hot, soft **mantle**. The mantle moves and carries the plates along with it.

The movement of plates can be **gradual** or sudden. When plates move suddenly, an earthquake happens. Part of the ground may lift up several feet, or cracks in the earth may appear. The place where Earth's crust breaks is called a **fault**.

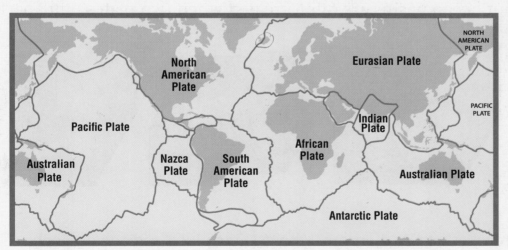

Earthquakes

Use the map to find where you live. Write the name of the plate you are on.

North American plate

Moving Plates

Earthquakes happen along the **boundaries** of plates, or where the edge of one plate meets another. Plates **interact** along their boundaries as they move in different directions.

Some plates slide past each other. The famous San Andreas Fault in California is an example of plates sliding in opposite directions. Other plates **collide**, or run into each other. When plates collide, they cause powerful earthquakes and can even build mountains. The Himalaya Mountains in Asia are the result of two plates colliding. In other places, plates move apart from each other. This does not cause very strong earthquakes, but ocean basins are often created when two plates pull apart.

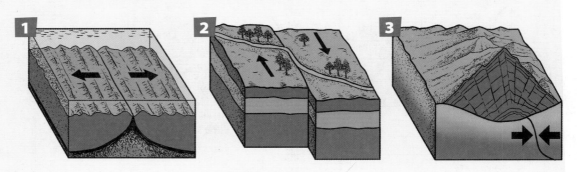

Write whether the diagrams above show plates *sliding past* each other, *colliding,* or *moving apart.*

1. _Moving apart_   3. _colliding_

2. _sliding past each one_

Concept:

Scientists use different tools to measure and classify earthquakes.

Measuring Earthquakes

Scientists study earthquakes with a tool called a **seismometer**, which detects and records movement in the ground. When an earthquake happens, a seismometer will display a series of zigzag lines that allow scientists to figure out the **duration** and strength of the quake.

In 1935, a scientist named Charles Richter invented a system of measuring earthquakes. This is called the Richter scale. An earthquake is given a number from 1 to 10 to describe its **magnitude**. A magnitude 1 earthquake is so weak that you can't feel it. An 8.0 earthquake would knock you off your feet! Since scientists began using the Richter scale, the strongest earthquake ever recorded was a 9.5 in Chile in 1960.

Write *true* or *false*.

1. A seismometer measures the magnitude of an earthquake.

         f

2. A magnitude 10 earthquake is the strongest.

         t

Earthquakes

Skill:

Interpret information in graphic representations.

Richter Scale

This chart shows the effects of earthquakes of different magnitudes around the world, as well as how many of them are recorded per year. Use the information in the chart to complete the sentences below.

Richter Scale Magnitude	Average Number of Earthquakes (per year)	Earthquake Effects
2.0–2.9	1,300,000	Not felt but are recorded on seismometers
3.0–3.9	130,000	Barely noticeable; hanging objects may swing
4.0–4.9	13,000	Most people notice them; buildings shake
5.0–5.9	1,300	Everyone notices them; windows may break
6.0–6.9	134	Walls may crack; chimneys may fall
7.0–7.9	18	Ground cracks; weak buildings fall down
8.0–8.9	1	Many buildings fall; bridges collapse
9.0–9.9	1 per 20 years	Complete devastation over a wide area
10.0+	Extremely rare	Never recorded

1. Earthquakes of a magnitude of 9.0 happen at a rate of about

   _____ every _____ years.

2. Usually, an earthquake must be at least a magnitude of _____ to cause any buildings to fall down.

3. Most people notice earthquakes that are a magnitude of _____ or greater.

4. The number of earthquakes between magnitudes of 3.0 and

   6.9 that happen every year is about _____.

Earthquakes Crossword Puzzle

Use the vocabulary words to complete the crossword puzzle.

| seismometer | duration | mantle | collide |
| boundary | interact | plates | fault |

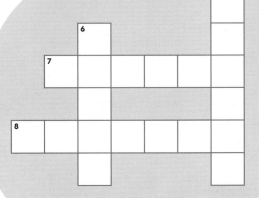

Across

5. to act on one another

7. a layer of molten rock beneath Earth's crust

8. to crash into

Down

1. a border or an edge

2. the length of time that something lasts

3. large sections of Earth's crust

4. a tool that records movements in Earth's crust

6. a break in Earth's crust where blocks of rock are moving in different directions

Earthquake-Proof

Engineers in areas where earthquakes happen must think about how to make buildings that can stand up to damage from a powerful quake. In this experiment, you will use the information on earthquake-proof designs to make two different buildings. You will then test how these buildings stand up against an earthquake.

What You Need

- toothpicks (at least 30)

- miniature marshmallows (at least 30)

- large baking dish

- 1 or 2 boxes of flavored gelatin (and help from an adult to make it)

- plastic wrap

Earthquake-Proof Design Tips

- Buildings with large, wide bases are stronger than those with small, narrow bases.

- Shorter buildings are more earthquake-proof than taller ones.

- Earthquake-proof buildings usually have cross-bracing, or triangle-shaped designs.

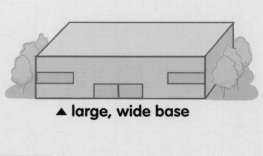

▲ large, wide base

◀ cross-bracing

Directions

1. Prepare the gelatin with an adult the night before the experiment, following the instructions. Pour the gelatin mixture into the baking dish so that it completely covers the bottom of the dish and is at least 1" thick.

2. Put plastic wrap on the baking dish and place it in the refrigerator.

3. The next day, use the marshmallows and toothpicks to create two different buildings: one that you think will stand up to an earthquake, and one that you think will fall down. Place them on top of the gelatin in the baking dish.

4. First, shake the baking dish back and forth slowly and softly. Next, shake it quickly and forcefully. Then answer the questions.

What Did You Discover?

1. What happened when you shook the dish softly? Did either of your buildings fall over? Which one seemed stronger?

   _____

   _____

2. What happened when you shook the dish harder? Did either of your buildings fall over? Which one seemed stronger?

   _____

   _____

3. What might you do to make your buildings stronger?

   _____

   _____

Earthquakes

Famous Earthquakes

There are many places on Earth where earthquakes happen often. Sometimes these earthquakes are so strong that they cause a lot of damage. People remember these earthquakes for years and years. Choose one of the areas below and research to find out about a famous earthquake that happened in that area. Then use the research to answer the questions.

| Japan | Alaska | California | Indonesia | Chile |

1. Where did the earthquake take place? _____

2. When did the earthquake take place? _____

3. What was the magnitude of the earthquake? _____

4. What effect did the earthquake have on the surrounding area? What type of damage did it do? Did it cause any other types of natural disasters (tsunamis, landslides, etc.)?

_____

_____

_____

_____

_____

_____

Earthquakes

Where Are Volcanoes?

Concepts:

There are three types of volcanoes: active, dormant, and extinct.

Most of the world's volcanoes are located along the edge of the Pacific Ocean.

Define It!

active: a volcano that is currently erupting, showing signs of erupting, or has erupted recently

dormant: a volcano that hasn't erupted recently, but is expected to erupt again

erupt: to release lava, ash, and gases

extinct: a volcano that will likely not erupt again

There are thousands of volcanoes on our planet. Most of them are **dormant** or **extinct**. This means that they haven't **erupted** for a long time, or they will not erupt again. However, about 1,500 volcanoes on Earth are still **active**. This means that they have erupted recently and could erupt again in the future.

Most of the world's active volcanoes are in an area called the Ring of Fire. The Ring of Fire is a band of volcanoes that circles the Pacific Ocean. These volcanoes are mostly located along the boundary of the Pacific Plate.

Answer the questions.

1. Where are most of the world's active volcanoes located?

   _____

2. About how many volcanoes on Earth are still active? _____

Concepts:

Hot molten rock beneath Earth's crust is called magma.

Hot molten rock after it erupts from a volcano is called lava.

Volcanoes

From Magma to Lava

Define It!

lava: hot melted rock that flows from a volcano

magma: hot melted rock that comes from Earth's mantle

vent: an opening in a volcano through which lava can flow

We may see volcanoes rise high above Earth's surface, but they also reach down into the middle layer of Earth, the mantle. Volcanoes form when hot rock rises from the mantle through cracks in the crust. The hot, soft rock of the mantle is always moving. As the rock gets closer to the crust, there is less pressure pushing against it. The rock begins to expand and turns from a solid into liquid **magma**.

When a volcano erupts, magma pushes up through a tube in the volcano and out of its **vent**. When magma reaches the surface, we call it **lava**. As lava cools, it turns from a liquid back into a solid. Now it is a hard rock, not soft the way it was in the mantle.

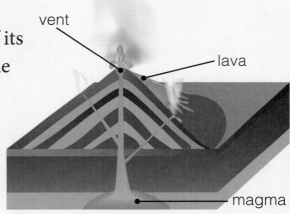

Composite Volcano

Write *true* or *false*.

1. Magma comes from the mantle. _____

2. As magma cools on Earth's surface, it becomes hard rock. _____

Ways Volcanoes Erupt

When volcanoes erupt, they can be either **violent** or quiet and steady. Quiet, steady eruptions are known as lava flows. Lava pours through a vent in the crust onto Earth's surface in a slow, constant stream. The Hawaiian Islands were created by this kind of eruption.

Mt. Bromo in Indonesia erupted violently in 2011.

Violent eruptions mostly happen in volcanoes that have a deep **chamber** that fills with magma. As magma fills the chamber, it releases gases. These gases build up under the layers of rock at the top of the volcano. Eventually, the pressure is so great that the volcano explodes, sending ash, gases, and other volcanic **debris** into the air. The eruption that destroyed the ancient city of Pompeii in Italy is an example of a violent eruption.

Lava flows slowly and steadily from Mt. Kilauea in Hawaii.

Write whether the sentence describes a *violent eruption* or a *quiet, steady* one.

1. Ash, gases, and debris explode into the air. _____

2. Lava oozes from the vent in a slow stream. _____

Volcanoes

Skills:

Interpret and identify information in graphic representations.

Volcano Variety

Study the chart to learn more about three different types of volcanoes.

Composite Volcano

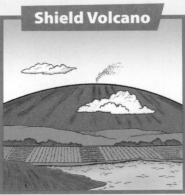

Shield Volcano

Cinder Cone

- tall and steep-sided
- formed from flows of sticky lava layered with other kinds of rocks
- can explode violently

- huge and dome-shaped
- formed from many layers of runny lava
- erupts quietly and often

- small and cone-shaped
- formed from blocks of cooled lava called cinders
- lava erupts in sprays

Write the name of the type of volcano being described.

1. has flows of thick, sticky lava _____

2. forms the smallest type of volcano _____

3. erupts with quiet, steady flows of lava _____

4. explodes violently _____

5. is formed from blocks of lava called cinders _____

6. has layers made from different kinds of rock _____

Volcanoes

Either/Or Questions

Write each answer.

1. If a volcano has erupted recently, is it active **or** extinct?

   _____

2. Is hot melted rock underneath Earth's crust called magma **or** lava?

   _____

3. Is magma stored in a volcano's vent **or** chamber?

   _____

4. Which one sends debris into the air—a violent eruption **or**
   a steady eruption?

   _____

5. Is a dormant volcano finished erupting **or** could it erupt again?

   _____

6. Does lava pour from a volcano's chamber **or** vent?

   _____

7. When a volcano erupts with lava flows, is it a violent eruption **or**
   a steady eruption?

   _____

Skills:

Conduct experiments and draw conclusions about the results.

Baking Soda Volcano

In this exciting experiment, you will make your own volcano and watch it erupt!

What You Need

- 6 cups (840 g) flour
- 2 cups (560 g) salt
- 4 tablespoons (60 mL) cooking oil
- 2 tablespoons (16 g) baking soda
- dishwashing detergent
- red food coloring

- vinegar
- 2 cups (450 mL) warm water
- bowl
- disposable baking pan
- 2-liter soda bottle (no cap)
- safety goggles

Directions

1. Mix the flour, salt, oil, and warm water in a bowl to make dough. The dough should be smooth and firm.

2. Stand the soda bottle in the middle of the baking pan. Mold the dough around the bottle in the shape of a cone volcano. Do not cover the bottle opening or drop any dough inside of it.

3. Fill the bottle most of the way full with warm water and add red food coloring.

4. Add 6 drops of the detergent to the bottle.

5. Add the baking soda to the bottle.

6. Slowly pour the vinegar into the bottle and watch what happens!

Shaping the Earth

What Did You Discover?

1. What happened when you added the vinegar to the contents in the bottle?

_____

_____

2. What part of the volcano did the soda bottle represent?

_____

3. What part of the volcano did the soda bottle opening represent?

_____

4. Before the water, food coloring, detergent, and baking soda left the bottle, what did they represent? Once they left the bottle, what did they represent?

_____

Volcanoes

Skill:

Write narratives to develop real or imagined experiences or events.

Volcano Alert!

Pretend that you live in a town near an active volcano. One morning, you wake up and see smoke coming out of the volcano's vent! Write a story about what happens next. Be sure to describe the type of volcano you live by. Use what you know about how different types of volcanoes erupt to tell your story.

_____

_____

_____

_____

_____

_____

_____

Volcanoes

About Waves

Concepts:

A wave is a disturbance that moves through a medium.

A wave carries energy from place to place.

Define It!

disturbance: something that moves another thing out of place

energy: the power to do work

medium: matter in which something is carried

A wave carries energy from one place to another. A wave is a **disturbance** that moves through matter such as air or water. The matter through which the wave moves is called the wave **medium**. A medium is something that carries another thing.

Energy creates the disturbance that makes a wave. The wave carries this energy from one place to another. For example, think of two people holding the ends of a rope stretched tightly between them. One person jerks her end of the rope up and back to its original position. The energy from the movement travels along the rope (the rope is the medium) in a wave to the other person. The rope moves up and down, but comes to rest in the same place. The rope doesn't move to another place, only the energy does.

Complete the sentences.

1. A wave carries _____energy_____.

2. A ____disturbance____ causes a wave.

3. A wave moves through a ____medium____.

What Is a Wave?

Wavelength

One way scientists measure waves is by **wavelength**. The highest point of a wave is the **crest**. A wavelength is the distance between one crest of a wave and the next crest. Waves with the longest wavelengths have the least energy. Waves with the shortest wavelengths have the most energy.

Energy from the sun travels to Earth in waves. These waves travel through empty space as well as through matter. Only some of the waves are **visible** to us. Visible light waves allow us to see the world around us.

Radio waves are not visible. They have long wavelengths and do not carry a lot of energy. They are used to send radio **signals**. **Microwaves** are shorter and carry more energy than radio waves do. Microwaves can reach into food and heat it. X-rays have a short wavelength. They can go through soft body parts to take pictures of bones and teeth.

Define It!

crest: the top part of something

microwave: an energy wave that is shorter than a radio wave

signal: a radio wave sent or received

visible: able to be seen

wavelength: the distance between one crest of a wave and the next

Write *radio wave, microwave,* and *x-ray* to complete the diagram of wavelengths.

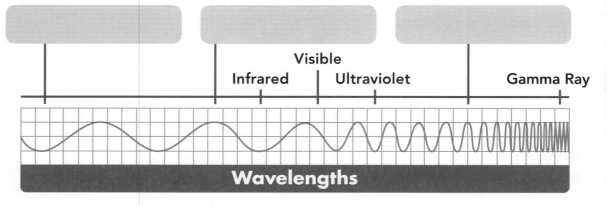

Visible

Infrared   Ultraviolet   Gamma Ray

Wavelengths

Amplitude of a Wave

Define It!

amplitude: the distance from a place of rest to the crest of a wave

decibel: a unit used to measure sound

Amplitude is another way scientists measure waves. This diagram shows a picture of a medium at rest (in green) with a wave moving through it. The amplitude of a wave is the distance from a place of rest to the crest of the wave.

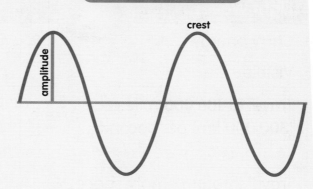

Wave Amplitude

Although sound waves are not visible, you can hear their amplitude. The louder the sound you hear, the greater the amplitude of the waves. Loudness is measured in **decibels**. The sound of leaves rustling in a breeze is about 10 decibels. The sound of a jet engine is about 140 decibels. Sounds above 85 decibels can harm your ears.

Circle the answers.

1. The louder the sound, the smaller the amplitude.   **true**   **false**

2. The sound of a jet engine can harm your ears.   **true**   **false**

3. Amplitude is measured from a place of rest
   to the crest of a wave.   **true**   **false**

Concepts:

Waves of the same type can differ in amplitude.

We can hear the amplitude of sound waves.

What Is a Wave?

Skill:

Use information gained from a table to demonstrate understanding and make comparisons.

What Is a Wave?

Comparing Waves

Light energy travels from your computer screen to your eyes as **light waves**. Sound energy travels from a guitar to your ears as **sound waves**.

Look at the table to find out how light waves and sound waves compare. Then answer the questions.

Light Waves	Sound Waves
Carry energy	Carry energy
Visible	Not visible
Travel at 186,000 miles (300,000 km) per second	Travel about 1,128 feet (343 m) per second, depending on the temperature of air
Travel through empty space or through a medium	Travel only through a medium
Wavelength, amplitude, and frequency can be measured	Wavelength, amplitude, and frequency can be measured

1. Which type of wave must have a medium? _____

2. Which type of wave travels faster? _____

3. Which type of wave can be seen with the human eye? _____

4. Explain one way in which the two wave types are alike.

   _____

   _____

   _____

   _____

Waves Crossword Puzzle

Use the vocabulary words to complete the crossword puzzle.

| amplitude | disturbance | medium | decibel |
| microwave | wavelength | visible | crest |

Across

1. matter in which something is carried

3. the top part of something

5. the distance from a place of rest to the crest of a wave

7. able to be seen

8. the distance between one crest of a wave and the next crest

Down

2. an energy wave that is shorter than a radio wave

4. something that moves another thing out of place

6. a unit used to measure sound

What Is a Wave?

Skills:

Follow a sequence of directions to complete a science demonstration.

Draw and write to demonstrate knowledge of a science topic.

What Is a Wave?

Making Waves

A wave carries energy from one place to another. Waves move through a medium. The medium can be a solid, a liquid, or a gas. Earthquakes are waves that move through the earth. Sound waves move through the gases that make up the air. Waves in the oceans and lakes move through liquid (water).

Learn about the energy of water waves by observing them with the following activities.

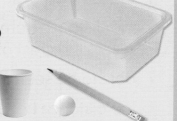

What You Need

- table tennis ball
- clear plastic container, such as a shoe storage box
- paper cup
- water
- pencil

Directions

1. Fill the plastic container with about 2" (5 cm) of water and let it rest.

2. Dip your finger into a cup of water. Let a drop of water fall from your finger into the plastic container to make water waves. Look closely to see the waves moving out in circles from the center where the drop of water falls. Looking into the container from the side, the waves look like this:

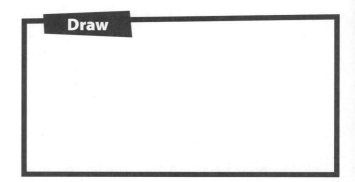

3. Draw a picture of what the waves look like from above.

Draw

4. Next, place the ball in the container of water near the middle and to one side. Then use your finger to disturb the water at one end of the container.

What Did You Discover?

1. Did the ball move horizontally from one end of the container to the other?   **yes   no**

2. Did the ball move up and down?   **yes   no**

The ball moved up and down in place. How can this be explained? Waves moved through the water, carrying *energy* from place to place. But the waves did *not* carry the water or the ball.

3. What did you learn?

_____

_____

_____

What Is a Wave?

What Is a Wave?

Catch a Wave

Complete the KWL chart. Write the name of a type of wave you would like to learn more about. Write what you already know in the **K** column. Write a question you have about this type of wave in the **W** column. Look in library books or on the Internet to find the answer. Write it in the **L** column.

Hint

Some waves you have learned about in this unit are visible light waves, radio waves, microwaves, x-rays, water waves, sound waves, and earthquake waves.

KWL Chart

Topic: _____ **Waves**

What I **K**now	What I **W**onder About	What I **L**earned

A Closer Look at Waves

Define It!

behave: to act in a certain way

bob: to move quickly up and down

observe: to watch

ripple: a small wave on the surface of water

shallow: not deep

Concepts:

Most waves are made when wind disturbs water.

Waves carry energy forward, but not water.

Waves in shallow water behave differently than deep-water waves.

Waves are created when energy disturbs the water in oceans and lakes. Most water waves are caused by wind blowing across the water's surface. This causes **ripples** that grow into waves when the wind catches them. The largest waves form in deep, open waters because that is where winds blow the strongest. Deep-water waves carry energy, but not water. If you could **observe** a single drop of water in a deep-water wave, you would see it **bob** up and down in a circle from the crest to the bottom of the wave. But the drop would not move forward!

Waves in **shallow** water near the shore **behave** differently, however. The bottom of the wave slows down as it drags on the ocean floor, while the crest of the wave races forward. The waves crash onto the shore, carrying water and leaving sand, stones, and shells there.

Waves in the Water

Answer the questions.

1. Why do the largest waves form in deep, open waters?

_____

2. How does the crest of a wave in shallow water behave?

_____

Concepts:

Tsunami waves are created by earthquakes.

People cannot eliminate natural hazards like tsunamis, but they can take steps to reduce their impact.

Waves in the Water

Tsunami

Define It!

earthquake: a shaking of the ground caused by rocks moving deep in the Earth

forecast: to tell ahead of time what will happen

seismic: having to do with earthquakes

tsunami: a very large ocean wave

Most **tsunami** waves are caused by **earthquakes**. The shaking energy of an earthquake pushes the water. Tsunami waves are much more powerful than ordinary water waves. They destroy buildings and take many lives. In deep ocean water, tsunami waves can be miles long, lifting the water up by about 3 feet (.9 m). These giant waves move at the speed of a jet plane. As the waves get nearer to land, they slow down and grow taller.

Scientists try to **forecast** when a tsunami will reach land. To do this, they use tools that measure **seismic** waves. Seismic waves are the shaking energy that moves through the earth during an earthquake. They tell scientists where and when earthquakes happen under the ocean. Scientists want to warn people to leave the area if a tsunami is approaching. In 2004, a tsunami was caused by a magnitude 9.0 earthquake under the Indian Ocean. Thousands of people in 14 countries lost their lives.

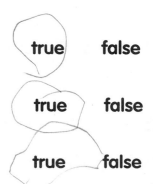

Circle the answers.

1. A tsunami wave is caused by wind.   **true**   false

2. Scientists want to forecast a tsunami in order to save lives.   **true**   false

3. Seismic waves are the shaking energy of an earthquake.   **true**   false

Wave Power

Define It!

electricity: a form of power

engineer: a person who plans things to be built

generator: a machine used to produce electricity

pollution: something dirty or harmful

Imagine that you are a surfer resting after a day in the ocean, floating on your surfboard. You can feel the energy of gentle waves as you bob up and down. Wave energy of water is always there, day and night. Scientists know there is a supply of energy in the ocean waves, and they are testing ways to use it.

There are powerful ocean waves along the coasts of Scotland and Portugal, and also along the coasts of Oregon and New Jersey in the United States. **Engineers** are working on ways to use the up-and-down motion of ocean waves to run **generators**. The generators produce **electricity** that could be used in homes. The engineers' challenge is to generate electricity in a way that will not cause **pollution** or harm life in the oceans.

**An Ocean Power Technologies PowerBuoy®
generating electricity from ocean waves.**

Complete the sentences.

1. Wave energy could be used to _____ for homes.

2. To generate electricity without causing harm is a challenge for

_____.

Waves in the Water

Skills:

Analyze and interpret information presented in a diagram.

Tsunami Safety

Tsunamis do not happen very often, but when they do, they are very dangerous. For your safety, know if you are in a tsunami area. If there is an earthquake, a tsunami could follow, so listen to a radio or TV for instructions. There may be as much as a two-hour warning or only minutes. Get to higher ground and go as far inland as you can.

Sometimes, people at the shore observe the water pulling back unusually far. This is called *draw back* and it can happen before a tsunami hits. People go toward the water to have a look. Do **not** do this! Run in the other direction, away from the water.

This diagram shows how a tsunami is caused by an earthquake. Label the *earthquake* and the *wave*.

This diagram shows how a tsunami hits the shore. Label the *draw back* and the *wave*.

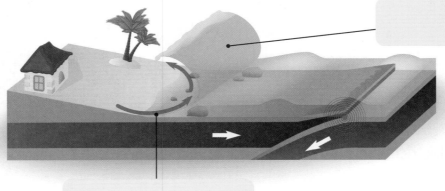

Waves in the Water

Either/Or Questions

Write each answer.

1. Is a ripple a small wave **or** a drop? _____

2. Do seismic waves move through air **or** earth? _____

3. Does a generator make electricity **or** ocean waves?

_____

4. Is a tsunami a type of wave **or** an earthquake? _____

5. Can electricity be forecast **or** generated? _____

6. Is it the job of an engineer to plan and test things **or**
to forecast things?

_____

7. To make a deep pool shallow, would you add water **or** take it out?

_____

8. Could a rubber ducky observe **or** bob? _____

Waves in the Water

Skills:

Develop a model to describe patterns in the movement of waves.

Measure and record patterns.

Waves in the Water

Measuring Waves

Do waves travel faster in deep or shallow water? A tsunami can move at 600 miles per hour in the open ocean, but it slows down as it nears the shore. Make a wave model to demonstrate the effect of the depth of water on the speed of waves.

What You Need

- 15" x 22" (38 cm x 56 cm) plastic storage container (under-the-bed height)

- 2 lengths of 2" x 4" (5 cm x 10 cm) wood: 1 short (5" or 13 cm) and 1 long (13" or 33 cm, slightly shorter than the width of the container)

- stopwatch
- ruler
- water
- blue food coloring
- a partner

Directions

1. Fill the container with water .8 inch (2 cm) deep. Mix in a few drops of blue food coloring.

2. Place the long piece of wood inside one end of the container to reflect the wave. Let the water settle.

3. Practice making a wave with the short piece of wood by pushing it into the water at the opposite end of the container and lifting it out. Watch the wave travel from one end of the container to the other.

4. Allow the water to settle. Work with a partner so one person can create the wave and the other can observe it closely.

5. Make a wave and time how long it takes to travel the distance to the long piece of wood. Record the time in the chart on page 81. Do this two more times.

6. Add water to the container until it measures 1.5 inches (4 cm) deep. Let the water settle. Then make a wave, time it, and record it three times.

7. Repeat this with water that is 2.4 inches (6 cm) deep.

Water Depth	Time
.8 in. (2 cm)	1. 2. 3.
1.5 in. (4 cm)	1. 2. 3.
2.4 in. (6 cm)	1. 2. 3.

Think About It

1. What pattern do you see in the results?

_____

_____

_____

2. Think about what you know about the speed of tsunami waves. Compare them to the results you found with your model.

_____

_____

_____

Waves in the Water

Apply What You Learned

Water waves are very powerful. They have the power to destroy or to be useful. Write to explain how this is so. Give examples.

Generating electricity with ocean waves.

Waves Can Be Natural Hazards

_____

_____

_____

_____

_____

Waves Can Be Useful to People

_____

_____

_____

_____

_____

Waves in the Water

Making Sound Waves

Concepts:

Sound waves result when an object vibrates.

Sound waves are made up of compressions and rarefactions of the air.

Define It!

compress: to squeeze or press

compression: an area where air is squeezed together

particle: a very small piece or speck

rarefaction: an area where air is not closely packed together

vibration: a quick back-and-forth motion

Sound waves are created when an object vibrates, or shakes. The **vibrations** move outward from the object. Sound waves can only move through a medium. They cannot exist in empty space. Most of the sounds we hear travel through air. However, sound waves can also travel through solids, liquids, and gases.

Think of a stretched rubber band. When it is plucked, it vibrates back and forth. As the rubber band moves, it pushes against the air and causes the air **particles** to **compress**, or squeeze together. **Compressions** are areas where the air particles are squeezed together. At the edges of the compressions are areas called **rarefactions** where the air particles are not as closely packed together. As more rarefactions and compressions form, they bump into more air and form waves. When the waves strike our ears, we hear sounds.

rarefactions

compressions

Sound Waves

Complete the sentences.

1. Sound waves are made when an object _____ .

2. Sound waves have rarefactions and _____ .

Concepts:

The faster an object vibrates, the greater its frequency.

A high-pitched sound has a higher frequency than a low-pitched sound.

Sound Waves

Frequency and Pitch

Sound waves are measured by their **frequency**. The frequency of a wave is the number of waves that pass a certain point, usually in one second. The faster an object vibrates, the greater its frequency. Frequency is measured in **hertz**. One hertz equals one wave per second.

Frequency and **pitch** go together. Pitch is the highness or lowness of a sound. A high-pitched sound, such as a whistle, has a higher frequency than a low-pitched sound, such as a big, deep drum.

Scientists talk about frequency, and **musicians** talk about pitch. A piano has 88 keys that play sounds from low-pitched to high-pitched. The lowest pitch is 28 hertz and the highest pitch is 4,186 hertz.

Circle the answers.

1. A high-pitched sound has a high frequency. **true** **false**

2. One wave per second equals one musician. **true** **false**

3. A hertz is a measure of sound wave frequency. **true** **false**

Acoustics

Define It!

acoustics: the study of sound

affect: to make a change in

architect: a person who plans buildings

decibel: a unit used to measure the loudness of sound

detect: to discover something

Sounds **affect** our lives in many ways every day. **Acoustics** is the study of sound. People may make acoustics their life's work if they are interested in how sound affects us. For example, some scientists study how to make the world quieter for people by making machines less noisy. Other scientists teach the dangers of loud sounds to people's hearing. Acoustical **architects** plan buildings that have safe **decibel** levels for people. Some scientists study how human-made sounds affect how ocean animals behave. Or they may use sound waves to locate and study fish. Some engineers create tools that use sound waves to help doctors **detect** or treat illnesses.

Concepts:

Acoustics is the study of sound and how it works.

A variety of science careers make use of acoustics.

Answer the questions.

1. List two things that can be made with quieter sound levels for people.

   _____

2. How can an architect help save people's hearing?

   _____

Safe Listening

The loudness of a sound is measured in decibels. Safe sound levels are below 85 decibels. Any noise at or above 85 decibels can harm our hearing over time. How can you protect your hearing from unsafe noise?

1. Turn down the sound.

2. Walk away from the sound.

3. Block the noise with earplugs or earmuffs.

Read the chart to discover the decibel levels of some common noises.

Is It Too Loud?

140–145	firecracker, jet taking off
130	stock car race
125	balloon popping
115	rock band, ambulance siren
110	car horn, baby crying
105	personal music player
100	snowmobile
90	power mower, food mixer
85	busy city traffic, school lunchroom
60–95	hair dryer
70	dishwasher
60	normal talking
20	whisper

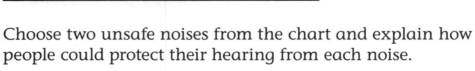

Choose two unsafe noises from the chart and explain how people could protect their hearing from each noise.

_____

_____

_____

_____

Sound Waves

Sound Waves Crossword Puzzle

Use the vocabulary words to complete the crossword puzzle.

| frequency | rarefaction | architect | musician |
| compression | acoustics | vibration | pitch |

Across

2. the study of sound

7. the highness or lowness of a musical sound

8. an area where air is not closely packed together

Down

1. an area where air is squeezed together

3. a person who has skill with music

4. a person who plans buildings

5. a quick back-and-forth motion

6. the number of sound waves that pass a given point in a given time

Sound Waves

Skills:

Construct
a model to
demonstrate
something in the
natural world.

Conduct
observational
testing of a
model.

Analyze and
interpret
patterns in data.

Changing Pitch

Pitch is the highness or lowness of a sound. A large, deep drum has a low pitch, and a whistle has a high pitch. Discover how to make sounds of different pitches with this activity.

What You Need

- foam cup
- 30-centimeter ruler
- masking tape
- rubber band, cut
- pencil
- small paper clip

Directions

1. Use the pencil tip to carefully poke a small hole in the bottom of the foam cup.

2. Thread the rubber band through the hole so that one end is inside the cup and the other is outside. Tape the outside end to the cup while you do the next step.

3. Tie the paper clip to the other end of the rubber band. Remove the tape and pull the rubber band so that the paper clip anchors it inside the cup as shown.

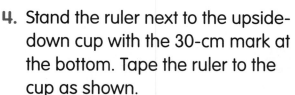

4. Stand the ruler next to the upside-down cup with the 30-cm mark at the bottom. Tape the ruler to the cup as shown.

5. Stretch the rubber band up and over the top of the ruler, and then tape it to the back of the ruler.

6. Hold the cup and pluck the rubber band three times.

Sound Waves

What Did You Discover?

1. What did you hear? _____

2. What did you see? _____

3. Press the rubber band to the ruler at the 2-cm mark and pluck it again. Repeat this at 4, 6, 8, and 10 cm on the ruler. How did the sound change when you pressed down on the rubber band?

   _____

4. By pressing down on the rubber band, you made the part that was able to vibrate shorter. The shorter the band, the faster it vibrated. What happened to the sound as the rubber band vibrated faster?

   _____

5. Predict what will happen to the sound if you start at 10 cm and go backward to 8, 6, 4, and 2 cm.

   _____

Complete the sentences. Use the words *higher, lower, faster,* and *slower.*

As the part of the rubber band that can vibrate becomes

shorter, the vibrations become _____. Faster vibrations

make the pitch _____.

As the vibrating part of the rubber band becomes longer,

the vibrations become _____. Slower vibrations make

the pitch _____.

Sound Waves

Waves

Skills:

Collect, record, and evaluate data.

Apply information gained from text in evaluating data.

Apply What You Learned

You might be surprised if you counted the number of sounds you hear in a day or even an hour. Make a list of the sounds you hear in the next 10 minutes. Using what you have learned, check the box next to each one that you think has a safe decibel level.

Hint

Safe sound levels are below 85 decibels. Normal talking is about 60 decibels. A school lunchroom is about 85 decibels. A personal music player is about 105 decibels.

☐ _____   ☐ _____

☐ _____   ☐ _____

☐ _____   ☐ _____

☐ _____   ☐ _____

☐ _____   ☐ _____

☐ _____   ☐ _____

☐ _____   ☐ _____

☐ _____   ☐ _____

Sound Waves

Telephone Basics

Concepts:

Digitized information can be sent over long distances.

A telephone converts the sound waves of a human voice to signals that can be sent along a wire.

Define It!

disconnect: to switch off

microphone: a tool for sending sound waves, using signals

network: a group of things connected to each other

signal: a pulse or beat of energy

switch: a tool for connecting

Before the telephone was invented, people could not speak to each other from a distance. Today we are able to talk to someone next door or a person on the other side of the world.

The basic parts of your home telephone are a **microphone**, a speaker, and a **switch**. The microphone changes the sound waves of your voice into **signals**. The signals are sent out through the wires in your home to **networks** of wires and radio waves that reach around the world. It all happens in an instant. When the person you are calling speaks back to you, your telephone's speaker goes to work. The speaker changes the signals coming from the other person's telephone into sound waves you can hear.

A switch connects your telephone to the wires when you answer your telephone. Then it **disconnects** your telephone from the network when you end your call.

microphone   speaker   switch

Complete the sentences.

1. A _____ changes sound waves into signals.

2. A _____ changes signals into sound waves you can hear.

Digital Waves

Concept:

High-tech devices such as cellphones can receive and decode information.

Digital Waves

Can You Hear Me?

Did you know that a **cellular** telephone, or cellphone, is really a type of radio? Cellphones are **wireless**, unlike many home telephones. When you make a call from a cellphone, signals travel by radio waves to a cellular tower. The cell tower picks up the calls from the radio waves. Most cell towers can pick up signals within 40 miles (64 km) around. This area around a tower is called a cell. The cells of several towers together form a **honeycomb** pattern across a city. When you travel out of **range** of a tower, your phone's signal gets weaker. The cell tower knows this, and sends your signal to a switching office. The switching office sends your call over to the next cell tower. If you ever travel outside the range of the towers, you cannot make a call.

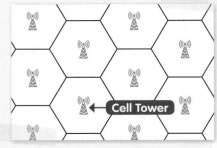

Cell Tower

Answer the questions.

1. How does a wireless call travel? _____

2. What does a switching office do?

_____

_____

Codes and Pixels

Define It!

digital: sending signals as a pattern of numerals

Internet: a system of computer networks around the world

pixels: tiny dots of light on a screen that form a picture

video: moving pictures

Concepts:

Digitized information can be transmitted over long distances.

High-tech devices such as computers can receive and decode information.

The telephone became very popular in the early 1900s. Back then, scientists worked on making a telephone with moving pictures, or **video**. Today, computers send and receive video, too. Computers use a network called the **Internet**.

The Internet is a **digital** network. Speech, writing, and video are changed to a code in order to be sent across the Internet. A digital code uses numerals to send signals. The digital code is sent through a giant network of wire cables and radio waves.

Digital pictures on a TV or a computer screen are made of tiny dots called **pixels**. The pixels are too tiny for you to see each one, but together they form pictures or video.

Circle the answers.

1. The Internet is a computer.　　　　　　true　　false

2. A digital code uses numerals to send signals.　　true　　false

3. Pixels are tiny dots on a computer screen.　　true　　false

Digital waves

Skills:

Analyze and interpret information presented in a diagram.

Develop a list using information presented in a diagram.

Stay Connected

Many people have a wireless network at home. A *router* uses radio waves to connect to things in the network. A *modem* connects the network to the Internet. Look at the diagram to find out more.

Read the diagram and answer the questions about it.

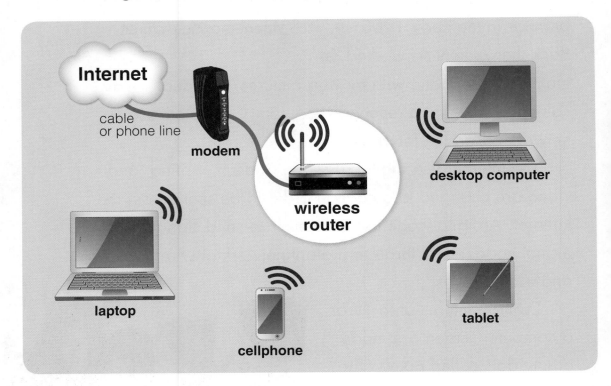

1. List the things that use the modem and router to help them connect to the Internet.

   _____

   _____

2. Describe the path that connects the Internet with the laptop.

   _____

   _____

Digital Waves

Either/Or Questions

Write each answer.

1. Are digital pictures made with a microphone **or** pixels? _____

2. Is a honeycomb a range **or** a pattern? _____

3. Is the Internet a network **or** a range? _____

4. Does a telephone have a pattern **or** a switch? _____

5. Can you hear a sound from a speaker **or** a pixel? _____

6. Does a digital code use numbers **or** letters? _____

7. Is a cellular phone soundless **or** wireless? _____

8. Is video moving air **or** moving pictures? _____

Digital Waves

Pictures in Code

Computers use numerals to send and receive pictures. The numerals are changed into pixels, or tiny dots on a computer screen. You can do this, too!

What You Need

- pencil
- graph paper (optional)

Directions

1. Look at the picture made of black and white squares below.

2. The numbers next to each row tell how the row is colored, starting at the left.

3. The first number tells how many white squares.

4. The next number tells how many black squares. The following number tells how many white, and so on.

5. Here is the tricky part: A zero at the beginning tells you that the row starts with a black square, and the number following zero tells how many squares should be black. Read the code and compare it to the picture.

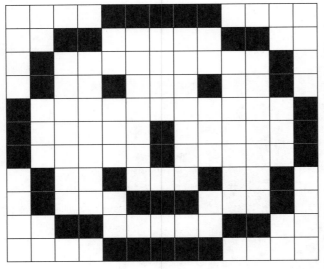

4, 5, 4
2, 2, 5, 2, 2
1, 1, 9, 1, 1
1, 1, 2, 1, 3, 1, 2, 1, 1
0, 1, 11, 1
0, 1, 5, 1, 5, 1
0, 1, 5, 1, 5, 1
1, 1, 2, 1, 3, 1, 2, 1, 1
1, 1, 3, 3, 3, 1, 1
2, 2, 5, 2, 2
4, 5, 4

6. Using a pencil, follow the number code to color the picture.

2, 1, 1, 2, 9

2, 2, 2, 1, 8

2, 1, 4, 1, 7

1, 1, 6, 1, 6

0, 10, 2, 1, 2

1, 1, 6, 1, 2, 3, 1

1, 1, 1, 2, 1, 1, 1, 1, 2, 3, 1

1, 1, 1, 2, 1, 1, 1, 1, 2, 3, 1

1, 1, 6, 1, 3, 1, 2

1, 1, 3, 2, 1, 1, 3, 1, 2

1, 1, 3, 2, 1, 1, 6

1, 8, 6

7, 1, 7

7, 8

7. Now plan and draw your own picture and write the code for it.

_____

_____

_____

_____

_____

_____

_____

_____

_____

_____

More Fun!

Use graph paper to create another picture. Write the code for it and give the code to a friend. Have your friend color the picture on another sheet of graph paper.

Digital Waves

Apply What You Learned

Pretend that your family is taking a road trip out west. Your dad wants to call your grandmother to tell her you will arrive tomorrow. But his cellphone won't make the call. Use what you know about cellphones, cellular towers, and networks to explain why.

_____

_____

_____

_____

_____

_____

_____

_____

Digital Waves

A Law of Energy

Define It!

conservation: saving the total amount of something

law: something that always happens under the same conditions

transfer: to move from one place to another

universe: all of matter and space

work: the use of force to move an object

Have you ever seen a bolt of lightning flash across the sky? Then you have seen a giant spark of energy. But what is energy? Scientists cannot say exactly what energy is. They do know some things about energy, however. Energy makes it possible to do **work**; that is, to cause something to move. It takes energy for you to run, and it takes energy for a car to move.

Scientists also know that energy can be neither created nor destroyed. This is known as the **law** of **conservation** of energy. If a girl runs across a soccer field and kicks a ball, the energy is **transferred** from the girl's body to the ball. The ball is set in motion. The energy is not lost. Scientists think that the total amount of energy in the entire **universe** always stays the same.

Circle the answers.

1. Energy cannot be transferred.   true   false

2. Energy cannot be destroyed.   true   false

3. When you kick a ball, the energy transfers to the ball.   true   false

4. Scientists know exactly what energy is.   true   false

What Is Energy?

What Is Energy?

Thinking About Energy

Scientists describe energy in two ways. **Potential** energy is stored energy. For example, the food you eat for breakfast gives you energy for your day. Energy from the food is stored up in your body. Your body uses the energy when you run a race or give someone a push on a swing at recess. A bowling ball lifted into the air has potential energy and so does a folded-up toy spring.

Kinetic energy is the energy of motion. An object that is moving from one place to another has kinetic energy. Think of a fast-moving car that **collides** with a road sign, knocking it over. The same car moving at a slow speed only bends the sign when they collide. This is because faster objects have more kinetic energy.

Write the answers.

1. What is another word for stored energy? _____

2. What is kinetic energy? _____

3. If Mason throws a fast snowball and Jake throws a slow one, whose snowball has more kinetic energy? _____

Energy on the Move

Define It!

electric current: the flow of electricity

generate: to make or create

power plant: a factory for generating power

vibrate: to move back and forth quickly

Energy can be transferred from place to place. One way this happens is through sound. A drummer striking a drum uses energy. Striking the drum causes it to move, or **vibrate**. This pushes the air around the drum, making sound waves. The sound waves transfer the sound energy to your ears.

Energy is also transferred by light. Light transfers energy from the sun at a high speed as light moves through empty space. The speed of light is about 186,000 miles per *second,* or about 300,000 kilometers per second. It only takes about 8 minutes and 20 seconds for light from the sun to reach you on Earth!

Energy can also be transferred by **electric current**. What happens when you plug in and turn on a toaster? Electric current **generated** by a **power plant** moves along wires to your home. The electric current flows to the toaster, supplying the energy the toaster needs to work.

List three ways that energy can be transferred from place to place.

1. _____

2. _____

3. _____

Concepts:
Energy can be transferred from place to place.

Energy is transferred through sound, light, and electric current.

We Use Energy

Think of the many things in a home that use some form of energy to make them work. *Appliances* such as refrigerators, washers, dryers, and dishwashers use energy. *Electronics* such as computers and televisions use it. Heating systems, air conditioners, and lights all use energy. This graph shows how energy is used in homes.

Read the graph and answer the questions.

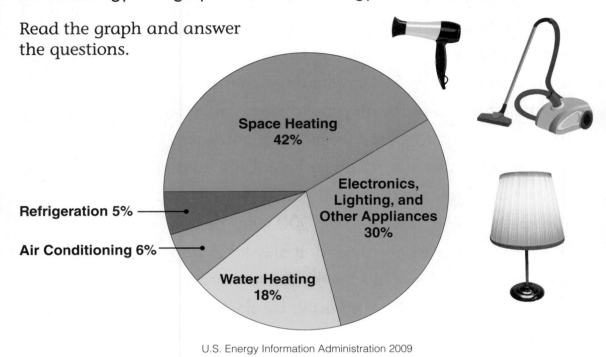

U.S. Energy Information Administration 2009

1. Which is used more—energy for heating or for cooling?

_____

2. What is 30% of the energy used for in homes?

_____

3. List in order the top three uses of energy in homes.

_____

_____

Energy Crossword Puzzle

Skill:
Apply content vocabulary.

Use the vocabulary words to complete the crossword puzzle.

| electric current | potential | transfer | collide |
| conservation | generate | kinetic | law |

Across

2. to bump into
3. the stored energy belonging to something
4. having to do with motion
6. saving the total amount of something
7. to move from one place to another
8. to make or create

Down

1. the flow of electricity
5. something that always happens under the same conditions

What Is Energy?

Can Energy Change Matter?

Learn about the changes that energy can make with this activity. Observe what happens to the white of an egg when you apply energy.

Note: Be careful when handling raw eggs. Eating uncooked eggs (or licking a beater) can make you sick. When you finish this activity, wash your hands and tools with soap and hot tap water.

What You Need

- white of an egg
- eggbeater or wire whisk
- bowl
- timer

Directions

1. Separate the egg white from the egg yolk. Put the egg white in a bowl. Look closely at the egg white. What color is it? How much does it fill the bowl? Does it look smooth and shiny? Record what you observe in the chart on page 105.

2. What will happen if you use energy to beat the egg white? Do you think the egg white will still be an egg white, or will it become a different thing? Write your prediction here.

_____

_____

3. Use an eggbeater to beat the egg. Put lots of energy into it! What happens? Record what you observe.

Time	Appearance of Egg White
Before beating	
After beating	
5 minutes later	
10 minutes later	
15 minutes later	
20 minutes later	
25 minutes later	

4. Do you think it is still an egg white after beating, or has it become a different thing? Give your reasons.

_____

_____

5. Let the egg white stand for 5 minutes. Then record what you observe in the chart. Do the same thing after 10, 15, 20, and 25 minutes.

6. Do you think that the matter that is left in the bowl after 25 minutes is the same matter you started with? Why?

_____

_____

Did You Know?

A *physical change* is any change in matter that does not produce new matter. You observed that the energy of beating the egg white changed the look of it, but it was still an egg white. If you repeat the steps, it will still be an egg white. The energy causes a physical change.

What Is Energy?

Skills:

Analyze and interpret visual images.

Write informative text to explain.

Apply What You Learned

Look closely at the two pictures. Describe what is happening in each picture. Then explain what type of energy is shown.

Hint

Potential energy is stored energy.
Kinetic energy is energy in motion.

Richard Paul Kane / Shutterstock.com

_____

_____

_____

_____

_____

_____

Richard Paul Kane / Shutterstock.com

_____

_____

_____

_____

_____

What Is Energy?

Concepts:

Heat energy flows from warm objects to cool ones.

When matter heats up, its molecules move faster.

Heat on the Move

Define It!

molecule: the smallest particle of matter

particle: a very small piece or speck

temperature: a measure of how hot or cold something is

Have you ever warmed your hands by the fire? Then you know something about heat energy. Heat from the fire flowed to your cold hands and warmed them up.

Heat energy moves between things that have different **temperatures**. What happens when an ice cube is added to a bowl of hot soup? Coldness from the ice cube does not flow to the soup. The soup cools because heat from the soup flows to the ice cube. Heat energy flows from warm objects to cool ones.

Matter is made up of tiny **particles** called **molecules**. When matter heats up, its molecules move faster. Temperature is a measure of the energy of this motion. Temperature tells how hot or cold something is.

Complete the sentences.

1. Heat energy flows from things that are _____

   to things that are _____.

2. When an object heats up, its molecules _____.

Heat Energy

Concepts:

Conduction is the transfer of heat when there is a difference in temperatures between objects.

A conductor is matter that transfers heat easily, such as metal.

Molecules in Motion

Define It!

conduction: the transfer of heat when there is a difference in temperatures

conductor: matter that provides an easy path for the flow of heat or other energy

transfer: to move from one place to another

Conduction is one way that heat energy is **transferred**. Conduction happens when two things are touching each other. For example, a metal spoon grows warm in a cup of hot tea. Why does this happen? When molecules bump into each other, heat energy is transferred. The heat moves from the faster-moving molecules of the hot tea to the slower-moving molecules of the cold spoon. The slower-moving molecules gain heat energy and speed up. Heat energy is transferred from one molecule to another until all the molecules in the tea and the spoon are moving at the same speed. The temperature of the tea and the temperature of the metal spoon become the same.

Metal is a good **conductor** because heat energy moves quickly through it. Cooking pots are metal because they quickly transfer heat energy from a stove to the food.

Answer the questions.

1. When the temperature of a cup of tea and the temperature of a spoon are the same, what do you know about their molecules?

   _____

2. What kind of heat transfer happens between food and a metal pan? _____

More About Heat

Convection is a second way that heat energy is transferred. Convection happens in liquids and gases, causing *convection currents*. Think of a pan of water on the stove. When the liquid gains heat energy, its molecules move faster and begin to spread out. When this happens, the heated liquid begins to rise. This causes **currents**, or flow, in the liquid. Currents formed in this way are called convection currents.

Radiation is a third way that heat is transferred. The sun is an example of radiation. The sun and other stars are always giving off energy. **Solar** energy travels to Earth through empty space in waves. Light waves, radio waves, and microwaves are some types of radiation from the sun.

Define It!

convection: the transfer of heat energy, causing movement in liquids and gases

current: a flow

radiation: the transfer of heat energy in waves

solar: from the sun

Concepts:

Convection is the transfer of heat through a liquid or gas, causing currents.

Radiation is the transfer of heat energy through waves.

Heat Energy

Circle the answers.

1. Molecules of a liquid spread out when they are heated. **true** **false**

2. Convection currents may form in liquids and gases. **true** **false**

3. Radiation does not transfer heat. **true** **false**

Energy

Skill:

Interpret information gained from text and apply it to a diagram.

Heat Energy

Heat and Weather

The sun's **radiation** warms the land on Earth. Then heat transfers from the land to the air by **conduction**. The air becomes warmer and lighter, so it rises. **Convection currents** begin to form. As the air goes higher into the sky, it begins to cool. When the air grows cool, it becomes heavier and sinks back toward land. Convection currents can cause breezes, winds, thunderstorms, and even hurricanes.

Label the diagram using the words *radiation, conduction,* and *convection currents*.

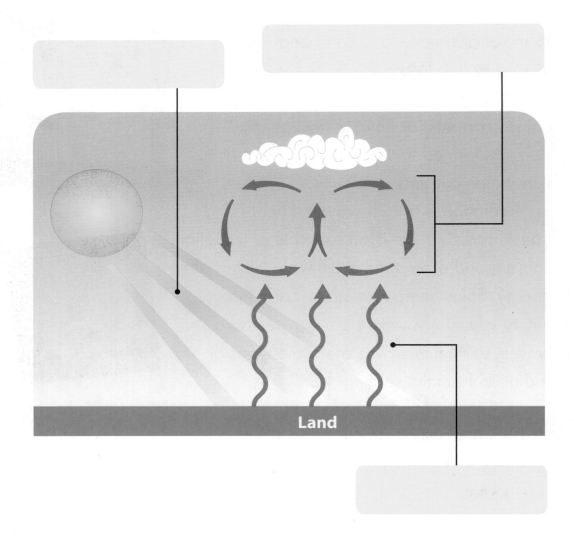

Either/Or Questions

Write each answer.

1. Are molecules particles of matter **or** empty space?

   _____

2. Is temperature a measure of how far away something is **or** how cold it is?

   _____

3. Does the sun's energy reach Earth by conduction **or** radiation?

   _____

4. Do currents cause breezes **or** radio waves? _____

5. Is metal a conductor **or** a current? _____

6. Does solar energy come from liquids **or** from the sun?

   _____

7. Does convection make currents **or** particles? _____

8. Does conduction happen when temperatures are the same **or** when they are different?

   _____

Heat Energy

Skills:

Plan and implement descriptive investigations to solve a specific problem in the natural world.

Answer questions and make inferences from observations.

Purple Swirl

To see the effects of heat transfer in action, all you need is food coloring and water. You can make the water swirl without even using your hands. Watch as heat energy does all the work!

What You Need

- clear plastic tray or rectangular container
- large foam cup filled with hot water
- large foam cup filled with ice water
- red and blue food coloring

Directions

1. Fill the tray with water that is almost warm.

2. Set the tray on top of the two cups, with the hot cup under one end and the cold cup under the other.

3. Add several drops of red food coloring to the water above the hot cup.

4. Add several drops of blue food coloring to the water above the cold cup.

5. Observe the movement of the coloring.

Heat Energy

What Did You Discover?

1. In what direction did the warmer red-colored water move?

_____

_____

2. Use what you know about the transfer of heat energy to explain why the water did this.

_____

_____

_____

3. What were the swirls of color that you observed?

_____

_____

4. What happened to the colors when you waited awhile longer?

_____

_____

5. What do you think is true about the temperature of all the molecules in the purple water?

_____

_____

Heat Energy

Apply What You Learned

Pretend that you are a molecule of water. One day, you are put into a soup pot on the stove. What happens next? Tell your story.

Hint

Heat energy makes molecules move faster and spread out. Convection currents begin to form when heated liquid rises.

_____

_____

_____

_____

_____

_____

_____

Making Electricity

Define It!

generator: a machine that produces electricity

hydroelectricity: electricity made from water power

rotor: part of a machine that turns

shaft: a long rod used in a machine

turbine: a machine with a wheel for making power

Concepts:

Turbines change kinetic energy of wind and water into electrical energy.

Hydroelectricity is created from the power of water.

Most electricity in the United States is made by power plants that burn natural gas, coal, and oil. But a small amount of the electricity we use comes from wind. Wind **turbines** change the kinetic energy of wind into electrical energy. Wind turns the giant turbine blades. The blades turn a **rotor** that turns a **shaft**. The shaft spins a **generator** that makes electric current. The electric current travels through wires to homes, schools, and other places.

Another small part of the electricity produced comes from the power of moving water. This is called **hydroelectricity**. (*Hydro* means "water.") Water falling over a dam has enough force to spin the blades of giant turbines. The energy of the turbines is changed into electricity.

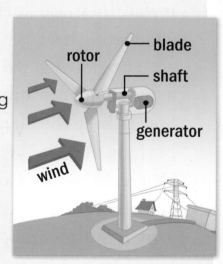

Write the answers.

1. What changes the kinetic energy of wind to electric current?

   _____

2. What changes the kinetic energy of water to electric current?

   _____

Electrical Energy

Electrical Energy

The Electric Toaster

An electric toaster is not as simple as it looks. When you push the **lever** down on a toaster, a switch completes a **circuit**. This sends electric current flowing through the toaster. Electric current flowing through a circuit can turn into heat. Inventors had a hard time figuring out how to make a toaster that wouldn't catch fire! They knew that electricity flows through conductors, such as metal. They also knew that some metals were not as good at conducting heat as others. Those metals are called **resistors**.

The glowing, red-hot **filaments** inside a toaster are resistors. The problem was how to keep the filaments from melting or burning. Albert Marsh solved the problem. He created a wire from two metals: nickel and chromium (KROH-me-uhm). The wire was a good resistor and could stand up to very high heat. This type of wire is still used in toasters today.

Complete the sentences.

1. A filament is a type of _____.

2. Electric current flows through a toaster when the _____ is complete.

Electricity and Light

Concepts:

Electric current creates light.

An LED display has bulbs in an electrical circuit.

Define It!

digital: showing time by displaying numerals (digits)

display: information shown on a screen

LED: a type of light used in many devices

segment: one part of something that has been divided

Long ago, people lit fires when night fell. Today we can flip a switch and electricity will travel through a circuit to give us light. An **LED** is one type of light. LEDs are all around us. For example, they form the lighted numbers on **digital** clocks. An LED is a tiny light bulb that fits into an electrical circuit. Each clock number is divided into seven parts, or **segments**. Each segment is an LED that is connected separately to the circuit. When one of the LEDs receives electric current, that segment lights up. The time displayed on the clock changes as segments are turned on and off. For example, when all seven of the LED segments in a number are turned on, the **display** shows the number 8. The clock has a counter that tells it when to change numbers and display the correct time.

Write *true* or *false*.

1. When electric current passes through an LED, sound is produced. _____

2. An LED display uses segments that light up. _____

Kinds of Energy

Electric currents can move energy from place to place. Electric currents produce heat energy in a toaster and light energy in an LED. They also produce the energy of motion in a fan and the energy of sound in a microphone.

For each picture, list one or more kinds of energy that are being produced from electric currents. Use the words *heat, light, motion,* and *sound.*

1	
2 Beep Beep 8:00	
3	
4	
5	
6	

Electrical Energy

Energy

Skill:
Apply content vocabulary.

Electrical Energy Crossword Puzzle

Use the vocabulary words to complete the crossword puzzle.

hydroelectricity	turbine	display	filament
segment	digital	resistor	circuit

Across

2. a machine for making power with a wheel

3. showing time by displaying numerals

5. a fine wire

6. one part of something that has been divided

7. information shown on a screen

8. a closed path or loop through which electricity can flow

Down

1. electricity made from water power

4. something that limits the flow of electric current

Electrical Energy

An Electromagnet

Electromagnets are used in electric motors. Many of the things you use every day have electromagnets—from doorbells to computers. You can demonstrate that a wire with electric current running through it creates a magnetic field. Make your own electromagnet!

Electrical Energy

What You Need

- 1.5 volt (AA) battery
- battery holder with clips
- 4 iron nails
- long insulated wire with stripped ends
- paper clips
- tape

Directions

1. Tape four iron nails together. Then wrap 10 coils of wire around the nails. Make sure that each coil of wire touches the next one. Leave some loose wire at the beginning and end.

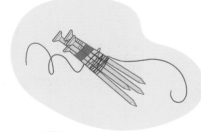

2. Place the battery in the holder. Attach both ends of the wire to the battery holder clips. This will make a circuit through which electric current can flow.

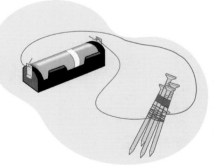

3. Bring the nails close to a pile of paper clips. What happens?

_____

_____

4. In the chart, record the number of paper clips that were affected by 10 coils.

Number of Coils of Wire	Number of Paper Clips Affected
10	
20	
30	
40	

5. Wrap the wire around the nails 10 more times. How many paper clips do the nails pick up now? Record the number.

6. Repeat Step 5 two more times, each time adding 10 more coils.

Important Note: Do not leave the circuit connected for very long, as it could cause the circuit to fail and the battery to die.

7. How did the number of coils of wire around the nails affect the strength of the electromagnet?

_____

_____

Electrical Energy

Skills:

Write explanatory text to convey information clearly.

Make a drawing and label it.

Apply What You Learned

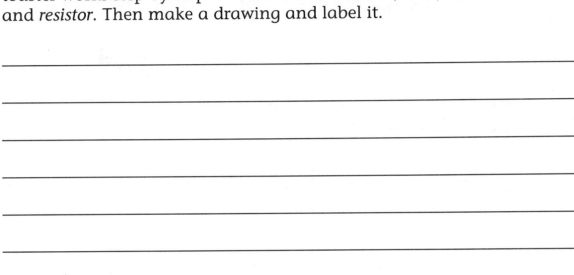

What is the science behind your breakfast toast? Explain how a toaster works step by step. Use the words *filament*, *lever*, *circuit*, and *resistor*. Then make a drawing and label it.

_____

_____

_____

_____

_____

_____

Draw

Electrical Energy

Light Travels

Concepts:

Visible light waves allow us to see the world around us.

Light travels through empty space at 186,000 miles per second.

Define It!

electromagnetic wave: a wave that travels at the speed of light

invisible: not able to be seen

laser: a tool that uses a strong beam of light

visible: able to be seen

The sun and other stars are always giving off energy in the form of **electromagnetic waves**. Light energy from the sun travels at 186,000 miles (300,000 km) per *second* through empty space to reach us on Earth. Other electromagnetic waves such as x-rays, radio waves, and microwaves are **invisible** to us. It is **visible** light that allows us to see the world around us. If you can see an object, that is because light is hitting the object and traveling to your eyes.

People have studied light for hundreds of years, but there is still a lot for scientists to wonder about. Scientists experiment with light to see how it behaves. This can help them to invent new uses for light. For example, a **laser** is a useful tool for doctors that uses a strong beam of light.

Answer the questions.

1. What is the only form of electromagnetic waves visible to us?

   _____

2. What is the speed of light traveling through empty space?

   _____

Light Energy

Concepts:

Light passes through transparent objects.

Translucent objects let some but not all light pass through.

Light cannot pass through opaque objects.

Light Energy

More About Light

Scientists sometimes talk about light as a **ray**, or a thin beam. Light rays move from place to place in a straight line. You see an object when light rays bounce off the object and travel to your eyes. Light rays pass through a **transparent** object, such as a window. **Translucent** objects let *some* light pass through, but not all. For example, sunglasses and tinted car windows are translucent. However, if a light ray hits an **opaque** object, such as a wall, it cannot pass through it. This is how shadows are made. When light can't pass through an object, a shadow is produced on the other side of the object.

Define It!

opaque: not allowing light to pass through

ray: a thin beam of light

translucent: allowing some light to pass through, but not all

transparent: allowing light to pass through

transparent ▶

▼ opaque

▲ translucent

◀ shadow

Write *true* or *false*.

1. You can see through opaque objects. _____

2. Light moves in a straight line. _____

3. Transparent objects make shadows. _____

How Does Light Behave?

Define It!

absorb: to soak up

reflect: to send light back from a shiny surface

reflection: an image made by reflecting light

refract: to bend a light wave

Opaque objects, such as walls, **absorb** light that tries to pass through them. This light energy can heat the objects that absorb it. This is why you can feel heat if you touch a brick wall on a hot, sunny day.

Some opaque objects are shiny, such as a mirror or a piece of metal. Shiny objects **reflect** most of the energy that strikes them. A small amount gets absorbed. The light bounces off them and travels in a new direction. Your eyes gather that light, and you see your **reflection**.

Sometimes, light passes through a transparent object and bends before it reaches your eyes. For example, light cannot pass from air through water in a straight line. Water **refracts**, or bends, the light. This is what happens when you look at a drinking straw in a glass of water. The water refracts the light rays, and your eye is tricked into thinking the straw is bent.

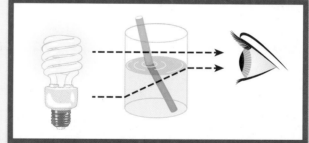

Concepts:

Light is absorbed by opaque objects.

Shiny objects reflect light.

Some objects refract, or bend, light.

Light Energy

Complete the sentences.

1. An opaque object that is shiny will _____.

2. When light bends as it passes through water, we can say the water

_____.

Skills:

Interpret and apply information gained from text and illustrations.

Light from the Sun

This picture shows some ways that sunlight affects us and our surroundings. Answer the questions to describe what you see.

1. Is the table *opaque*, *transparent*, or *translucent*?

_____

2. Are the sunglasses *opaque*, *transparent*, or *translucent*?

_____

3. Which objects are reflecting light? Name at least two.

_____

_____

4. Which objects are absorbing light? Name at least two.

_____

_____

5. Which objects show light being refracted? Name two.

_____

_____

Skill Sharpeners—Science • EMC 5324 • © Evan-Moor Corp.

Light Energy

Light Energy Crossword Puzzle

Use the vocabulary words to complete the crossword puzzle.

| transparent | laser | absorb | refract |
| translucent | opaque | reflect | ray |

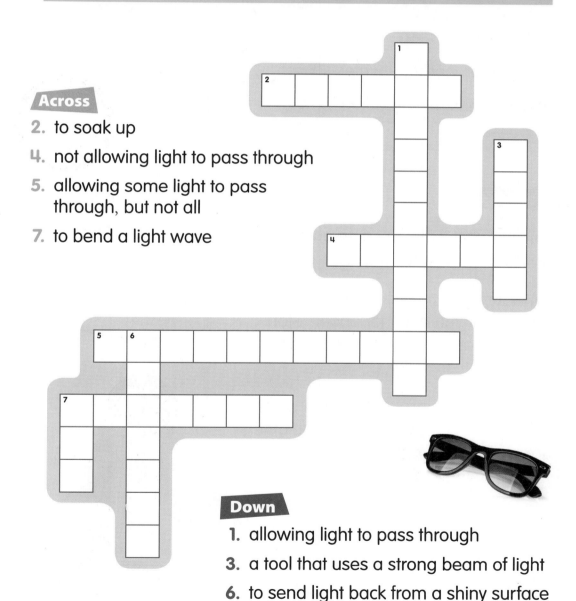

Across

2. to soak up

4. not allowing light to pass through

5. allowing some light to pass through, but not all

7. to bend a light wave

Down

1. allowing light to pass through

3. a tool that uses a strong beam of light

6. to send light back from a shiny surface

7. a thin beam of light

Light Energy

Skills:

Follow a sequence of directions to conduct a science investigation.

Record observations and interpret results.

Sunlight and Heat Energy

On a hot and sunny summer day, do you feel cooler in the sun or the shade? Do you feel cooler in light-colored clothing or dark-colored clothing? Find out what this has to do with the energy in sunlight.

What You Need

- 2 clear jars of the same size, with lids

- room-temperature water

- black construction paper

- white construction paper

- rubber bands or clear tape

- 2 thermometers

- clock

Directions

1. Fill both jars with the same amount of room-temperature water.

2. Measure and record the temperature of the water in each jar under "Start" on the chart on page 129. Also record the time.

3. Put the lids on the jars. Cover one jar and lid with black paper and the other jar and lid with white paper. Use rubber bands or tape to secure the paper.

Light Energy

	Time						
	Start						
Temperature in Black Jar (ºC)							
Temperature in White Jar (ºC)							

4. Place the jars in sunlight. Predict what will happen to the temperature of the water in the two jars.

_____

5. Measure and record the water temperature and the time every 5 to 10 minutes. Move the jars if necessary to keep them in the sunlight.

6. What happened to the water temperature in the jars?

_____

7. Which jar of water got warmer?

_____

_____

_____

8. What heated the water in the jars?

_____

9. From what you observed, which color paper absorbs more light energy?

_____

Light Energy

Skills:

Apply scientific knowledge to writing a narrative about an imagined experience.

Use descriptive details.

Apply What You Learned

KENNY TONG / Shutterstock.com

Wow!

Albert Einstein was a famous scientist who did "thought experiments." In one, he imagined what he would see if he were riding on a beam of light.

Imagine your own thought experiment with light. Would you travel from the sun to Earth? Would you travel through something transparent or translucent? Would you be absorbed by something opaque? Tell your story. Show what you have learned about how light behaves.

_____

_____

_____

_____

_____

_____

_____

_____

_____

_____

_____

_____

Light Energy

Answer Key

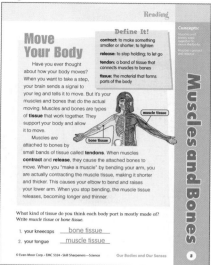

Move Your Body

Define It!
contract: to make something smaller or shorter; to tighten
release: to stop holding; to let go
tendon: a band of tissue that connects muscles to bones
tissue: the material that forms parts of the body

Have you ever thought about how your body moves? When you want to take a step, your brain sends a signal to your leg and tells it to move. But it's your muscles and bones that do the actual moving. Muscles and bones are types of **tissue** that work together. They support your body and allow it to move.

Muscles are attached to bones by small bands of tissue called **tendons**. When muscles **contract** and **release**, they cause the attached bones to move. When you "make a muscle" by bending your arm, you are actually contracting the muscle tissue, making it shorter and thicker. This causes your elbow to bend and raises your lower arm. When you stop bending, the muscle tissue releases, becoming longer and thinner.

What kind of tissue do you think each body part is mostly made of? Write *muscle tissue* or *bone tissue*.

1. your kneecaps   bone tissue
2. your tongue   muscle tissue

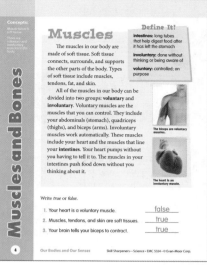

Muscles

Define It!
intestines: long tubes that help digest food after it has left the stomach
involuntary: done without thinking or being aware of
voluntary: controlled; on purpose

The muscles in our body are made of soft tissue. Soft tissue connects, surrounds, and supports the other parts of the body. Types of soft tissue include muscles, tendons, fat, and skin.

All of the muscles in our body can be divided into two groups: **voluntary** and **involuntary**. Voluntary muscles are the muscles that you can control. They include your abdominals (stomach), quadriceps (thighs), and biceps (arms). Involuntary muscles work automatically. These muscles include your heart and the muscles that line your **intestines**. Your heart pumps without you having to tell it to. The muscles in your intestines push food down without you thinking about it.

The biceps are voluntary muscles.

The heart is an involuntary muscle.

Write *true* or *false*.

1. Your heart is a voluntary muscle.   false
2. Muscles, tendons, and skin are soft tissues.   true
3. Your brain tells your biceps to contract.   true

Bones

Define It!
cartilage: a hard tissue found in parts of the body such as the ear, nose, and joints
rigid: unable to bend

The bones in our body are made of hard tissue. Hard tissue protects parts of the body and provides support. For example, the bones of your ribcage protect your lungs and heart. Your femur, or highbone, provides support for the muscles in your upper leg. Bones and **cartilage** are two types of hard tissues in humans. Some animals have other types of hard tissue such as antlers or shells.

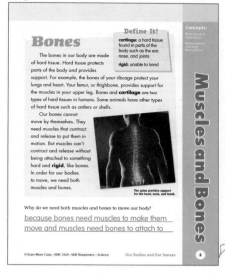

Our bones cannot move by themselves. They need muscles that contract and release to put them in motion. But muscles can't contract and release without being attached to something hard and **rigid**, like bones. In order for our bodies to move, we need both muscles and bones.

The spine provides support for the head, neck, and trunk.

Why do we need both muscles and bones to move our body?
because bones need muscles to make them move and muscles need bones to attach to

---

Visual Literacy

Function and Form

Look at the pictures of different muscles and bones in the body. Then mark an X in the box of the correct answer for each question.

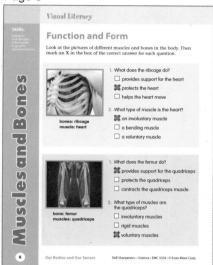

bones: ribcage
muscle: heart

1. What does the ribcage do?
   ☐ provides support for the heart
   ☒ protects the heart
   ☐ helps the heart move

2. What type of muscle is the heart?
   ☒ an involuntary muscle
   ☐ a bending muscle
   ☐ a voluntary muscle

bone: femur
muscles: quadriceps

3. What does the femur do?
   ☒ provides support for the quadriceps
   ☐ protects the quadriceps
   ☐ contracts the quadriceps muscle

4. What type of muscles are the quadriceps?
   ☐ involuntary muscles
   ☐ rigid muscles
   ☒ voluntary muscles

Vocabulary Practice

Either/Or Questions

Write each answer.

1. Is a contracted muscle shorter and thicker or longer and thinner?
   shorter and thicker

2. Does your brain tell voluntary muscles to move or do they move automatically?
   your brain tells them

3. Is muscle tissue hard or soft?   soft

4. Do tendons connect bones to other bones, muscles to other muscles, or muscles to bones?
   muscles to bones

5. Is hard tissue bendable or is it rigid?   rigid

6. Is the heart or the biceps an involuntary muscle?   heart

7. When you release a muscle, are you tightening it or letting it go?
   letting it go

8. Is cartilage considered a hard tissue or a soft tissue?
   hard tissue

Muscles Work in Pairs, continued

6. Place Tube 1 and Tube 2 together as shown. Then stretch the rubber bands of Tube 1 down to the bent ends of the paper clip of Tube 2 and loop them around. Wrap masking tape around Tube 2 to cover the bent ends of the clip.

7. Tape one rubber band to the cardboard tube "lower arm" as shown. Tape the other rubber band to the back of the ball as shown.

8. Bend and straighten the model arm and notice what happens to the rubber bands.

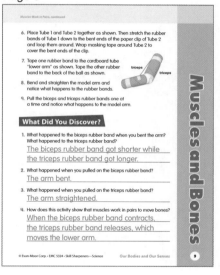

biceps
triceps

9. Pull the biceps and triceps rubber bands one at a time and notice what happens to the model arm.

What Did You Discover?

1. What happened to the biceps rubber band when you bent the arm? What happened to the triceps rubber band?
   The biceps rubber band got shorter while the triceps rubber band got longer.

2. What happened when you pulled on the biceps rubber band?
   The arm bent.

3. What happened when you pulled on the triceps rubber band?
   The arm straightened.

4. How does this activity show that muscles work in pairs to move bones?
   When the biceps rubber band contracts, the triceps rubber band releases, which moves the lower arm.

Application

Move It or Lose It

Simple exercises can help you think about how muscles are responsible for movement. Perform each exercise below, and then write down which muscles you think you were using. Use the diagram to help you name the muscles.

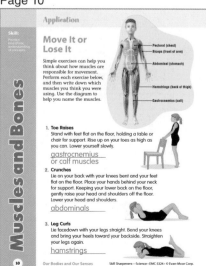

Pectoral (chest)
Biceps (front of arm)
Abdominal (stomach)
Hamstrings (back of thigh)
Gastrocnemius (calf)

1. **Toe Raises**
   Stand with feet flat on the floor, holding a table or chair for support. Rise up on your toes as high as you can. Lower yourself slowly.
   gastrocnemius or calf muscles

2. **Crunches**
   Lie on your back with your knees bent and your feet flat on the floor. Place your hands behind your neck for support. Keeping your lower back on the floor, gently raise your head and shoulders off the floor. Lower your head and shoulders.
   abdominals

3. **Leg Curls**
   Lie facedown with your legs straight. Bend your knees and bring your heels toward your backside. Straighten your legs again.
   hamstrings

Reading

Tissues of the Skin

Define It!
connective tissue: tissue that provides structure and support to the body
epithelial tissue: tissue that covers the inside and outside surfaces of the body
organ: a group of tissues that perform specific functions
temperature: a measure of the heat of a person's body

You may not think of your skin as an **organ**, but it is. In fact, it is the largest organ of your body. Your skin keeps your body from drying out. It also helps to keep your **temperature** constant and blocks disease.

Skin is made up of two types of tissue: **epithelial tissue** and **connective tissue**. Connective tissue supports and connects other tissues in the body. But when you look at your skin, you are seeing epithelial tissue. Epithelial tissue protects the body from the outside world. It keeps the body from losing fluids. It also releases sweat, which keeps us cool.

Name three things that epithelial tissue does.   Examples:

1. protects the body from the outside world
2. keeps the body from losing fluids
3. releases sweat

Layers of the Skin

Define It!
dermis: the middle layer of skin
epidermis: the outer layer of skin
hypodermis: the bottom layer of skin

There are three layers of skin. The bottom layer is called the **hypodermis**. The hypodermis is a layer of fat and connective tissue that helps connect the skin to muscles and bones.

epidermis
dermis
hypodermis

The middle layer of skin, the **dermis**, is made mostly of connective tissue. The dermis includes hair roots, nerve endings, and sweat glands. The dermis cushions the body and controls body heat. It also allows us to feel pain, temperature, and pressure.

The top layer of skin is called the **epidermis**. The epidermis is made of epithelial tissue. It protects the other layers of your skin and prevents your body from losing water.

Answer the questions.

1. Which layer of skin is the bottom layer?   hypodermis
2. Which layer protects the other layers of skin?   epidermis
3. Which layer contains hair roots?   dermis

Page 13

Concepts: ...

Callus and Sebum

Define It!
callus: a dry, tough layer of skin
friction: the rubbing of one object against another
sebum: an oily substance that covers the epidermis

The epidermis layer of skin helps to protect the body. But what protects the epidermis? Sometimes, layers of tough and dry tissue form on the epidermis to keep the skin from getting damaged. When there is a lot of **friction** on your skin, the layers of tissue build up to become thick and hard. This is what we call a **callus**. Calluses most often develop on the feet and hands.

An oily substance called **sebum** also protects your skin. Sebum acts like a natural waterproof seal. It keeps your skin from absorbing too much water. Sebum also helps keep water inside the skin so it doesn't dry out.

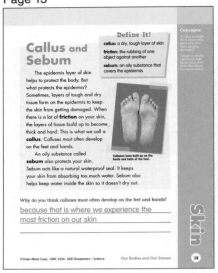
Calluses have built up on the heels and balls of the feet.

Why do you think calluses most often develop on the feet and hands?
<u>because that is where we experience the most friction on our skin</u>

Page 14

Skills: ...

Visual Literacy

The Three Layers

Look at the diagram of the three layers of skin. Label the *dermis*, *epidermis*, and *hypodermis*.

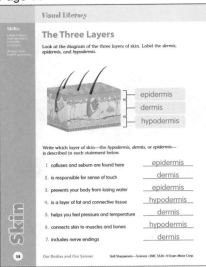
- epidermis
- dermis
- hypodermis

Write which layer of skin—the *hypodermis*, *dermis*, or *epidermis*—is described in each statement below.

1. calluses and sebum are found here — epidermis
2. is responsible for sense of touch — dermis
3. prevents your body from losing water — epidermis
4. is a layer of fat and connective tissue — hypodermis
5. helps you feel pressure and temperature — dermis
6. connects skin to muscles and bones — hypodermis
7. includes nerve endings — dermis

Page 15

Vocabulary Practice

Skin Crossword Puzzle

Use the vocabulary words to complete the crossword puzzle.

dermis   callus   connective   epidermis
sebum   epithelial   organ   friction

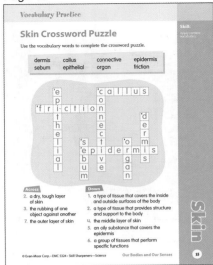

Across
2. a dry, tough layer of skin
3. the rubbing of one object against another
7. the outer layer of skin

Down
1. a type of tissue that covers the inside and outside surfaces of the body
2. a type of tissue that provides structure and support to the body
4. the middle layer of skin
5. an oily substance that covers the epidermis
6. a group of tissues that perform specific functions

Page 16

Skills: ...

Hands-on Activity

What Do You Feel?

In this experiment, you will test your skin's ability to feel differences in temperature.

What You Need
- 3 tall glasses of water: 1 with hot tap water, 1 with room-temperature water, 1 with ice water
- stopwatch to time yourself

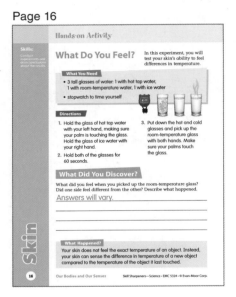

Directions
1. Hold the glass of hot tap water with your left hand, making sure your palm is touching the glass. Hold the glass of ice water with your right hand.
2. Hold both of the glasses for 60 seconds.
3. Put down the hot and cold glasses and pick up the room-temperature glass with both hands. Make sure your palms touch the glass.

What Did You Discover?
What did you feel when you picked up the room-temperature glass? Did one side feel different from the other? Describe what happened.
<u>Answers will vary.</u>

What Happened?
Your skin does not feel the exact temperature of an object. Instead, your skin can sense the difference in temperature of a new object compared to the temperature of the object it last touched.

Page 17

Hands-on Activity

Skills: ...

Sense of Touch

Is your skin equally sensitive all over your body? Try this experiment to find out.

What You Need
- ruler
- a partner
- 2 toothpicks

Directions
1. Explain to your partner that you will lightly touch him/her with either one or two toothpicks. Make sure your partner keeps his/her eyes closed.
2. Without telling your partner, hold two toothpicks so that the points measure .25 inch (.6 cm) apart and touch him/her on the fingertip. Ask your partner if he/she felt one or two points. If he/she says one, separate the two toothpicks so that they are .5 inch (1.3 cm) apart and touch him/her again.
3. Repeat this exercise by moving the toothpicks farther and farther apart until your partner feels two points. Mark an **X** on the chart at the measurement where he/she felt two points. Repeat Steps 2 and 3 with the other body parts given on the chart.

	.25 in. (.6 cm)	.5 in. (1.3 cm)	.75 in. (2 cm)	1 in. (2.5 cm)
Fingertip				
Upper Arm				
Back				

What Did You Discover?
Answers will vary— Examples:
1. Which part of your partner's body was most sensitive? Explain why.
<u>fingertip, because she felt two points at .25 in (.6 cm) apart</u>
2. Which part of your partner's body was least sensitive? Explain why.
<u>back, because she didn't feel the two points until they were 1 in. (2.5 cm) apart</u>

Page 18

Skill: ...

Application

Protect Your Skin

Name some of the ways that your skin protects your body. Then write about the ways that your body protects your skin. Include information about what happens in the different layers of the skin.
<u>Answers will vary but should include how the dermis cushions the body and controls sensations of pain and pressure; how the epidermis protects the other layers of skin and prevents the body from losing water; how a callus protects skin against friction; and how sebum keeps the body from absorbing too much water and/or the skin from drying out.</u>

Make Connections
What are some things you do to protect and take care of your skin?
<u>Answers will vary but might include wearing sunscreen, putting on lotion, and/or washing off dirt with soap.</u>

Page 19

Reading

Concepts: ...

Parts of the Eye

Define It!
iris: the colored part of the eye that controls the amount of light that can enter
pupil: the dark circle in the center of the iris where light enters the eye
sclera: the white part of the eye that controls movement
spherical: shaped like a ball or globe

Have you ever wondered how you are able to see? Our eyes are the organs that control our sense of sight. They take in light and send signals to the brain. The brain then tells us what we are seeing.

Even though eyes may appear circular or almond-shaped, they are really **spherical**. The parts of the eye that we can see are the **sclera**, **iris**, and **pupil**. The sclera is the white part of the eye. It contains muscles that control the eye's movement. The iris is the colored part of the eye. It controls the amount of light that can enter the eye. The pupil is the dark circle in the center of the iris. Light enters the eye through the pupil.

Optic Nerve — Sclera — Cornea — Lens — Pupil — Iris — Retina

Answer the questions.
1. What shape are our eyes? — spherical
2. Which part of the eye controls its movement? — sclera

Page 20

Concepts: ...

Light Enters the Eye

Define It!
cornea: the clear layer forming the front of the eye
reflect: to throw back heat, light, or sound without absorbing it
refract: to change the direction of light

To see the world around you, your eyes need light. Eyes send your brain information about an object's shape, color, and movement. They do this by taking in light that **reflects** off that object. Light reflected off an object travels in a straight line into your eye.

Light enters the eye through the **cornea**. The cornea is a clear coating that covers the iris and pupil at the front of the eye. It helps to **refract**, or change the direction of the light. It also helps the eye to focus. Light travels through the cornea to the pupil. When it is very bright and there is a lot of light, the pupil is small. When it is dark, the pupil grows larger in order to let more light into the eye.

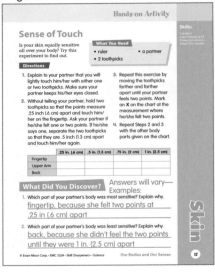

Write *true* or *false*.
1. Light travels in a straight line into the eye. — true
2. The pupil grows larger when it is bright out. — false
3. The cornea helps to refract light. — true

Page 21

Concepts: ...

How We See

Define It!
lens: the part of the eye that focuses and refracts light
optic nerve: nerves that send signals from the eye to the brain
project: to cause light to appear on a surface
retina: a layer at the back of the eye that changes images into nerve signals

After light passes through your pupil, it travels to the **lens**. The lens helps to focus the light to a part on the back of the eye called the **retina**. Because the lens refracts light, the image **projected** to the retina is upside down! The retina's job is to change the projected image into nerve signals. These signals are sent through the **optic nerve** to the brain. The brain is then able to make sense of what you are seeing.

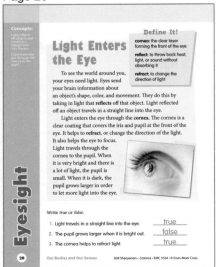

Say you are looking at a tree. In an instant, you are able to tell that it is a tree because light reflected off the tree and traveled in a straight line into your pupil. The lens refracted the light and projected the image to your retina. The retina changed the image into nerve signals, which traveled along the optic nerve to your brain. Then your brain told you, "It's a tree!"

Complete the sentences.
1. The <u>optic nerve</u> sends signals to the brain.
2. The lens projects an image onto the <u>retina</u>.

Page 22

Visual Literacy

Skills: Interpret and identify information in graphic representations

The Eyes Have It

Look at the numbered diagram of the eye. Next to each matching number and description below, label the *cornea, iris, lens, optic nerve, pupil, retina,* and *sclera.*

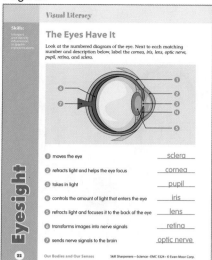

1. moves the eye — sclera
2. refracts light and helps the eye focus — cornea
3. takes in light — pupil
4. controls the amount of light that enters the eye — iris
5. refracts light and focuses it to the back of the eye — lens
6. transforms images into nerve signals — retina
7. sends nerve signals to the brain — optic nerve

Eyesight

22 | Our Bodies and Our Senses | Skill Sharpeners—Science • EMC 5324 • © Evan-Moor Corp.

Page 23

Vocabulary Practice

Skill: Apply science vocabulary

Either/Or Questions

Write each answer.

1. Is the pupil **or** the iris the colored part of the eye? — iris

2. Does the lens take in **or** refract light? — refract

3. Is the sclera the white part **or** the colored part of the eye? — white part

4. Is the eye circular **or** spherical in shape? — spherical

5. Is an image projected **or** reflected onto the retina? — projected

6. Does the cornea **or** the optic nerve send signals to the brain? — optic nerve

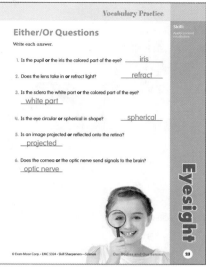

Eyesight

© Evan-Moor Corp. • EMC 5324 • Skill Sharpeners—Science | Our Bodies and Our Senses | 23

Page 25

Blind Spot, continued

6. Using the ruler, draw a straight line through the center of the dot and the **X** to both edges of the card.

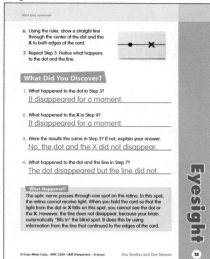

7. Repeat Step 3. Notice what happens to the dot and the **X.**

What Did You Discover?

1. What happened to the dot in Step 3?
   It disappeared for a moment.

2. What happened to the **X** in Step 4?
   It disappeared for a moment.

3. Were the results the same in Step 5? If not, explain your answer.
   No, the dot and the X did not disappear.

4. What happened to the dot and the line in Step 7?
   The dot disappeared but the line did not.

What Happened?

The optic nerve passes through one spot on the retina. In this spot, the retina cannot receive light. When you hold the card so that the light from the dot or **X** falls on this spot, you cannot see the dot or the **X.** However, the line does not disappear, because your brain automatically "fills in" the blind spot. It does this by using information from the line that continued to the edges of the card.

Eyesight

© Evan-Moor Corp. • EMC 5324 • Skill Sharpeners—Science | Our Bodies and Our Senses | 25

Page 26

Application

Skill: Answer text-based questions

Out of Sight

Choose an object in your room and focus on it. Now answer the questions to describe how you are able to see this object.

1. What is the object? Answers will vary.

2. How does light enter your eye from the object?
   Light reflects off the object and enters my eye in a straight line.

3. Through which two parts of the eye does light enter?
   cornea and pupil

4. Which part of the eye refracts the light onto the retina?
   lens

5. How does the image of your object appear on your retina?
   upside down

6. What is the retina's job?
   to change the image into nerve signals

7. Which part of the eye sends nerve signals to the brain?
   optic nerve

8. What happens when nerve signals reach your brain?
   your brain tells you what you are seeing

Eyesight

26 | Our Bodies and Our Senses | Skill Sharpeners—Science • EMC 5324 • © Evan-Moor Corp.

Page 27

Reading

Concepts: Objects make sound by vibrating to produce sound waves. The human ear detects vibrations. The faster the vibration, the higher the pitch of the sound.

What Is Sound?

Your ears are amazing organs. They pick up all the sounds around you and tell your brain what you are hearing. They also help you keep your balance! But to understand how your ears work, you first need to understand what sound is.

Objects make sounds by **vibrating**, or moving quickly back and forth. These vibrations produce **sound waves** that move just like ripples in water. The highness or lowness of a sound is called the **pitch**. The faster an object vibrates, the higher the pitch of the sound. The slower an object vibrates, the lower the pitch of the sound. People can hear a wide range of sounds—from a low, deep drum to a high-pitched whistle and from a quiet whisper to loud rock music.

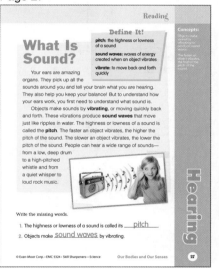

Define It!

pitch: the highness or lowness of a sound

sound waves: waves of energy created when an object vibrates

vibrate: to move back and forth quickly

Write the missing words.

1. The highness or lowness of a sound is called its — pitch

2. Objects make — sound waves — by vibrating.

Hearing

© Evan-Moor Corp. • EMC 5324 • Skill Sharpeners—Science | Our Bodies and Our Senses | 27

Page 28

Concept: The pinna collects sound waves and helps to determine the direction of sound.

Outer Ear

The ear is made up of three different sections: the outer ear, middle ear, and inner ear. The **pinna** is the part of the outer ear that you can see. The main job of the pinna is to collect sound waves. The shape and position of the pinna helps you to determine the direction of a sound. If a sound is coming from behind you or above you, it will bounce off the pinna in a different way than if it is coming from in front of you or below you. Because the pinna faces forward, you can hear sounds better in front of you than you can behind you.

The outer ear also includes the **ear canal**. This is where **earwax** is produced. Earwax fights dirt that could hurt the skin inside the ear canal. Earwax also collects dirt to help keep the ear canal clean.

Define It!

ear canal: a long tube that runs from the outer ear to the middle ear

earwax: the waxy matter produced in the ear canal

pinna: the part of the ear you can see

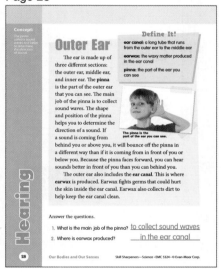
The pinna is the part of the ear you can see.

Answer the questions.

1. What is the main job of the pinna? — to collect sound waves

2. Where is earwax produced? — in the ear canal

Hearing

28 | Our Bodies and Our Senses | Skill Sharpeners—Science • EMC 5324 • © Evan-Moor Corp.

Page 29

Concepts: The eardrum turns sound waves into vibrations that are sent to the inner ear. The inner ear translates vibrations into nerve signals the brain can interpret as sound.

Middle and Inner Ear

After sound waves enter the outer ear, they travel through the ear canal into the middle ear. The middle ear's main job is to turn those sound waves into vibrations and send them to the inner ear. To do this, the middle ear needs the **eardrum**, which is a thin piece of tightly stretched skin. The eardrum separates the outer ear from tiny bones in the middle ear. When sound waves pass through the eardrum, they vibrate the bones in the middle ear before entering the inner ear.

The vibrations enter the inner ear through the **cochlea**. The job of the cochlea is to change sound vibrations into signals the brain can understand. The cochlea is filled with liquid, which ripples like a wave when the bones of the middle ear vibrate. These "waves" send out signals that the brain **interprets** as sound.

Define It!

cochlea: a curved part of the inner ear that turns vibrations into signals

eardrum: a thin skin in the middle ear that vibrates when sound waves move through it

interpret: to make sense of

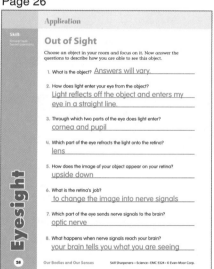

Write *true* or *false*.

1. The cochlea changes vibrations into signals. — true
2. The eardrum is located in the inner ear. — false

Hearing

© Evan-Moor Corp. • EMC 5324 • Skill Sharpeners—Science | Our Bodies and Our Senses | 29

Page 30

Visual Literacy

Skill: Label images that represent scientific concepts

Parts of the Ear

Look at the diagram of the ear. Label the *cochlea, ear canal, eardrum,* and *pinna.*

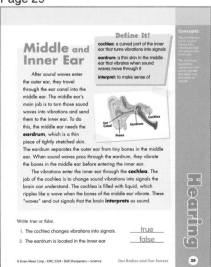
cochlea
ear canal
pinna
eardrum

Fill in the blanks to describe the path that sound waves take through the ear.

Sound waves enter the ear through the — pinna

They travel through the ear canal to the — eardrum

Sound waves vibrate tiny — bones — in the middle ear before entering the inner ear through the — cochlea — . The cochlea changes the sound vibrations into — signals — the brain then — interprets — as sound.

Hearing

30 | Our Bodies and Our Senses | Skill Sharpeners—Science • EMC 5324 • © Evan-Moor Corp.

Page 31

Vocabulary Practice

Skill: Apply content vocabulary

Hearing Crossword Puzzle

Use the vocabulary words to complete the crossword puzzle.

cochlea	sound waves	vibrate	pinna
eardrum	interpret	pitch	ear canal

Across

3. the part of the ear you can see
5. to move back and forth quickly
6. a part of the inner ear that changes sound vibrations into signals
7. a membrane in the middle ear that vibrates in response to sound waves
8. the highness or lowness of sound

Down

1. waves of energy created when an object vibrates
2. a long tube that runs from the outer ear to the middle ear
4. to make sense of

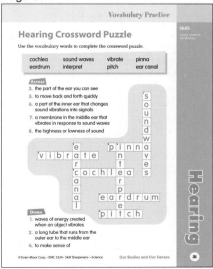

Hearing

© Evan-Moor Corp. • EMC 5324 • Skill Sharpeners—Science | Our Bodies and Our Senses | 31

Page 33

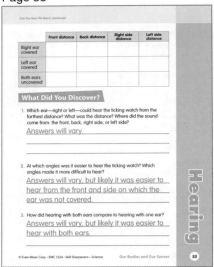

	Front distance	Back distance	Right side distance	Left side distance
Right ear covered				
Left ear covered				
Both ears uncovered				

What Did You Discover?

1. Which ear—right or left—could hear the ticking watch from the farthest distance? What was the distance? Where did the sound come from: the front, back, right side, or left side?

   Answers will vary.

2. At which angles was it easier to hear the ticking watch? Which angles made it more difficult to hear?

   Answers will vary, but likely it was easier to hear from the front and side on which the ear was not covered.

3. How did hearing with both ears compare to hearing with one ear?

   Answers will vary, but likely it was easier to hear with both ears.

© Evan-Moor Corp. • EMC 5324 • Skill Sharpeners—Science   Our Bodies and Our Senses   33

Hearing

Page 34

Application

Skill: Write sentences to develop and comprehend integrated improvements in science

Catch a Sound Wave

Pretend that you are a high-pitched sound wave. Describe your journey through the ear and how you think the person acted when he or she heard your sound.

Hint

Choose one of these sounds, or use your own idea:
- a whistle
- tires screeching
- an opera singer's voice

An object makes sound waves when it vibrates. The faster it vibrates, the higher the pitch of the sound.

Answers will vary but should demonstrate an understanding of pitch and the parts of the ear.

Hearing

34   Our Bodies and Our Senses   Skill Sharpeners—Science • EMC 5324 • © Evan-Moor Corp.

Page 35

Reading

Concept: Weathering and erosion help to shape the planet's surface.

Shaping Our Planet's Surface

Earth's surface is made up of many **landforms**. These landforms include mountains, valleys, islands, and canyons. The landforms on Earth have been shaped and reshaped by natural forces. Two of the most important forces in shaping our planet's surface are **weathering** and **erosion**.

Weathering is the breaking down or wearing away of rocks by water or wind. Have you ever picked up a very smooth rock on the beach? The smoothness of the rock is a result of the weathering waves of the ocean and the wind blowing on the beach. Erosion is the moving of rocks and soil by water, wind, ice, or **gravity**. High waves on a beach can erode sand dunes, carrying the sand back into the ocean.

Define It!

erosion: the moving of rocks and soil by water, wind, ice, or gravity

gravity: a force that pulls objects toward the center of Earth

landform: a natural feature of Earth's surface

weathering: the breaking down or wearing away of rocks by water or wind

Name one example of weathering and one example of erosion from the text.

1. weathering: waves and wind make rocks smooth

2. erosion: high waves erode sand dunes

© Evan-Moor Corp. • EMC 5324 • Skill Sharpeners—Science   Shaping the Earth   35

Weathering & Erosion

Page 36

Concept: Over millions of years, layers of sediment become layers of rock.

Layers of Rock

One of Earth's most **spectacular** natural features is the mile-deep Grand Canyon in northern Arizona. It is also one of the best examples of weathering and erosion. Visitors can look from the rim of the canyon to see the Colorado River far below. The walls of the canyon have many layers of different kinds of rock. Some of the rocks are as much as two billion years old!

Over millions of years, small pieces of sand called **sediment** were **deposited** in the area where the Grand Canyon formed. As new layers of sediment were deposited, the older layers were pressed down. Over time, they became solid layers of rock. But it wasn't until five or six million years ago that weathering and erosion began cutting into the rock to form the canyon.

Define It!

deposit: to put or set something down in a specific place

sediment: very small pieces of sand and minerals set down by water, wind, or ice

spectacular: beautiful in an eye-catching way

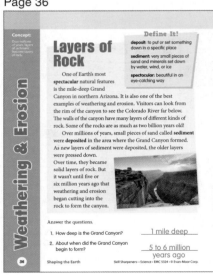

Answer the questions.

1. How deep is the Grand Canyon?   1 mile deep

2. About when did the Grand Canyon begin to form?   5 to 6 million years ago

Weathering & Erosion

36   Shaping the Earth   Skill Sharpeners—Science • EMC 5324 • © Evan-Moor Corp.

Page 37

Shaping the Grand Canyon

Five or six million years ago, the Grand Canyon began to take shape. When rain fell, water ran down the **sloping** land of the Rocky Mountains. This eroded the soil, making **channels**. Over time, the channels became the path for the Colorado River. Over millions of years, the Colorado River kept eroding the soil and carving out the canyon.

Weathering also helped form the canyon. Rainwater ran into cracks in the rocks and froze in the winter. When the water froze, it **expanded** and pushed the rocks apart. Gravity caused sections of the canyon wall to fall, making the canyon wider. Wind also shaped the canyon. Bits of sand, blown by wind, chipped away at the canyon walls and weathered the rock. All these forces are at work even today, and they continue to change the canyon.

Define It!

channels: cuts in the ground made by moving water such as a river or stream

expand: to become larger

sloping: slanting; on an angle

Concept: Erosion and weathering helped form the Grand Canyon.

5 million years ago

Today

Circle all of the things that helped to shape the Grand Canyon.

(gravity)   earthquakes   (wind)

(rainwater)   mudslides   (ice)

© Evan-Moor Corp. • EMC 5324 • Skill Sharpeners—Science   Shaping the Earth   37

Weathering & Erosion

Page 38

Skills: Interpret and identify information in photographs.

Visual Literacy

Weathered Rock

Look at the pictures of the rocks. On the lines below, describe what each rock looks like. Write down their colors, textures, and shapes. Then tell which one you think has been more weathered and why.

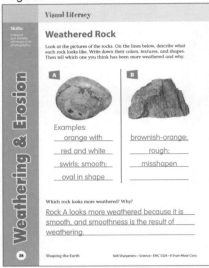

A   B

Examples:

| orange with red and white swirls; smooth; oval in shape | brownish-orange; rough; misshapen |

Which rock looks more weathered? Why?

Rock A looks more weathered because it is smooth, and smoothness is the result of weathering.

Weathering & Erosion

38   Shaping the Earth   Skill Sharpeners—Science • EMC 5324 • © Evan-Moor Corp.

Page 39

Vocabulary Practice

Skill: Apply content vocabulary.

Weathering/Erosion Crossword Puzzle

Use the vocabulary words to complete the crossword puzzle.

spectacular   landform   channels   sloping
weathering   sediment   erosion   expand

Across

3. a natural feature of Earth's surface

4. cuts in the ground made by moving water

8. the moving of rocks and soil by water, wind, ice, or gravity

Down

1. slanting; on an angle

2. the breaking down or wearing away of rocks by water or wind

5. to become larger

6. beautiful in an eye-catching way

7. very small pieces of sand and minerals set down by water, wind, or ice

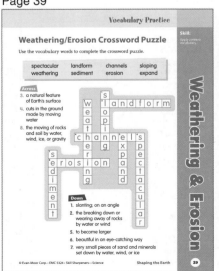

Weathering & Erosion

© Evan-Moor Corp. • EMC 5324 • Skill Sharpeners—Science   Shaping the Earth   39

Page 40

Hands-on Activity

Skills: Conduct experiments and draw conclusions about the results.

Home Erosion

Have you ever made a sand castle on the beach? Chances are, it wasn't very long before the castle was knocked down. What might make your sand castle stronger? And how does erosion affect sand castles or other structures made of sand and soil? Find out in this experiment.

What You Need
- sand
- soil
- 2 buckets
- 4 plastic cups
- portable fan (with batteries)
- garden hose with sprayer

Directions

1. Before you start the experiment, look at the sand and soil. How do they feel? Do the sand and soil stick together easily, or do they fall apart? Record your observations.

Chart 1	Description
Sand, before experiment	
Soil, before experiment	

2. Make a prediction. Which structure do you think will stay standing longer—one made of dry sand or one made of dry soil? Explain your answer.

   the best guess is the soil structure, because soil sticks together better

3. Pack one plastic cup with dry sand and turn it upside down on the ground in order to make a structure. Repeat the same thing with another plastic cup and the dry soil.

Weathering & Erosion

40   Shaping the Earth   Skill Sharpeners—Science • EMC 5324 • © Evan-Moor Corp.

Page 41

4. Create mud by mixing some of the soil with water in one bucket. In the other bucket, create wet sand by mixing some of the sand with just enough water to make it stick together.

5. Now make two more structures, one with mud and one with wet sand.

6. Blow on each of the structures one at a time, using the fan. Record what you observe in Chart 2.

7. Reusing the plastic cups, make four more structures by repeating Steps 3, 4, and 5.

8. Holding the hose, stand about 2 feet from your structures. Spray all the structures for about 30 seconds and then turn off the sprayer. Record what you observe in Chart 2.

Chart 2	Dry Soil	Dry Sand	Mud	Wet Sand
Wind (fan)				
Water (hose)				

Answers will vary— Examples:

What Did You Discover?

1. Which structure fell down first to the fan? Which stood up the best?

   likely the dry sand fell down first; the mud withstood the wind

2. Which structure stood up best against the water?

   likely the mud structure

Weathering & Erosion

© Evan-Moor Corp. • EMC 5324 • Skill Sharpeners—Science   Shaping the Earth   41

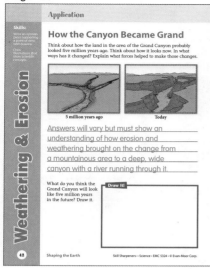

Weathering & Erosion

Skills:
Write an opinion piece supporting a point of view with reasons.

Draw illustrations that show scientific concepts.

Application

How the Canyon Became Grand

Think about how the land in the area of the Grand Canyon probably looked five million years ago. Think about how it looks now. In what ways has it changed? Explain what forces helped to make those changes.

5 million years ago | Today

Answers will vary but must show an understanding of how erosion and weathering brought on the change from a mountainous area to a deep, wide canyon with a river running through it.

What do you think the Grand Canyon will look like five million years in the future? Draw it.

Draw It!

42   Shaping the Earth   Skill Sharpeners—Science • EMC 5324 • © Evan-Moor Corp.

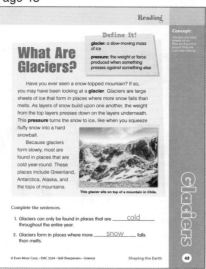

Reading

What Are Glaciers?

Define It!

glacier: a slow-moving mass of ice

pressure: the weight or force produced when something presses against something else

Have you ever seen a snow-topped mountain? If so, you may have been looking at a **glacier**. Glaciers are large sheets of ice that form in places where more snow falls than melts. As layers of snow build upon one another, the weight from the top layers presses down on the layers underneath. This **pressure** turns the snow to ice, like when you squeeze fluffy snow into a hard snowball.

Because glaciers form slowly, most are found in places that are cold year-round. These places include Greenland, Antarctica, Alaska, and the tops of mountains.

This glacier sits on top of a mountain in Chile.

Complete the sentences.

1. Glaciers can only be found in places that are ___cold___ throughout the entire year.

2. Glaciers form in places where more ___snow___ falls than melts.

Concept: Glaciers are large masses of ice that are found in places that are cold year-round.

Glaciers

© Evan-Moor Corp. • EMC 5324 • Skill Sharpeners—Science   Shaping the Earth   43

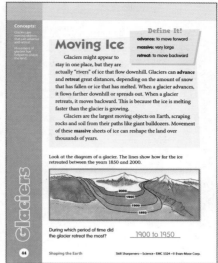

Glaciers

Concepts: Glaciers are moving objects that advance and retreat. Movement of glacier ice has helped to shape the land.

Moving Ice

Define It!

advance: to move forward

massive: very large

retreat: to move backward

Glaciers might appear to stay in one place, but they are actually "rivers" of ice that flow downhill. Glaciers can **advance** and **retreat** great distances, depending on the amount of snow that has fallen or ice that has melted. When a glacier advances, it flows farther downhill or spreads out. When a glacier retreats, it moves backward. This is because the ice is melting faster than the glacier is growing.

Glaciers are the largest moving objects on Earth, scraping rocks and soil from their paths like giant bulldozers. Movement of these **massive** sheets of ice can reshape the land over thousands of years.

Look at the diagram of a glacier. The lines show how far the ice retreated between the years 1850 and 2000.

During which period of time did the glacier retreat the most? ___1900 to 1950___

44   Shaping the Earth   Skill Sharpeners—Science • EMC 5324 • © Evan-Moor Corp.

Glaciers Shape the Land

Define It!

basin: a large hole in the ground that can contain water

debris: small pieces of rock

moraine: a ridge of loose rock and soil created by a glacier and left behind when the glacier melts

ridge: a long and narrow raised area

One way that glaciers shape the surface of our planet is by erosion. The ice carries broken rocks and soil over long distances and deposits the **debris** far from its original location. One of the best examples of this kind of erosion is California's Yosemite Valley. Huge glaciers carved a giant U-shaped valley in the rock and left behind **ridges** of dirt and gravel called **moraines**.

In other places, erosion by glaciers created lakes. The Great Lakes were formed from **basins** scooped out by moving glaciers. When the ice melted, these basins filled with water.

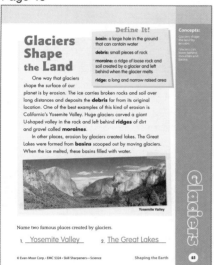

Yosemite Valley

Name two famous places created by glaciers.

1. ___Yosemite Valley___   2. ___The Great Lakes___

Concepts: Glaciers shape the land by erosion. Glaciers can leave behind moraines and basins.

Glaciers

© Evan-Moor Corp. • EMC 5324 • Skill Sharpeners—Science   Shaping the Earth   45

Visual Literacy

Skill: Label images that represent scientific concepts.

Moraines and Basins

Look at the diagram. Label the *glacier*, *moraines*, and *basin*.

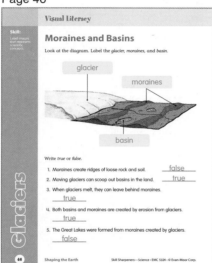

glacier

moraines

basin

Write *true* or *false*.

1. Moraines create ridges of loose rock and soil. ___false___

2. Moving glaciers scoop out basins in the land. ___true___

3. When glaciers melt, they can leave behind moraines. ___true___

4. Both basins and moraines are created by erosion from glaciers. ___true___

5. The Great Lakes were formed from moraines created by glaciers. ___false___

Glaciers

46   Shaping the Earth   Skill Sharpeners—Science • EMC 5324 • © Evan-Moor Corp.

Vocabulary Practice

Either/Or Questions

Skill: Apply content vocabulary.

Write each answer.

1. Is something that is massive very large or very small?
   ___very large___

2. When a glacier moves backward, is it advancing or retreating?
   ___retreating___

3. Were the Great Lakes formed from basins or moraines?
   ___basins___

4. Does pressure from the weight of the snow or erosion of the land help to form glaciers?
   ___pressure___

5. Is debris deposited by mountains or by glaciers?
   ___glaciers___

6. When a glacier flows farther downhill, is it retreating or advancing?
   ___advancing___

7. Are moraines large holes in the ground or ridges of dirt and gravel?
   ___ridges of dirt and gravel___

Glaciers

© Evan-Moor Corp. • EMC 5324 • Skill Sharpeners—Science   Shaping the Earth   47

Grinding Glaciers, continued

	Observations
Ice cube on foil	foil scratched and tore
Ice cubes in tub	ice melted and left sand behind

What Did You Discover?

1. What happened when you rubbed the ice cube across the foil?
   It scratched or tore the foil.

2. What was left in the plastic tub after the ice cubes melted? What would this be called when a real glacier melts?
   water and sand; a moraine

3. What did the experiment show you about the ways that glaciers change Earth's surface?
   Glaciers can move rock, and these rocks can scratch and reshape Earth's surface.

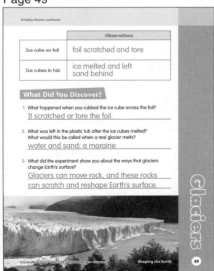

Glaciers

© Evan-Moor Corp. • EMC 5324 • Skill Sharpeners—Science   Shaping the Earth   49

Application

Skill: Write an opinion piece supporting a point of view with reasons.

Melting Ice

Today we live in a very warm period, and glaciers are on the move—backward! Most glaciers are melting faster than they are growing, and this has scientists worried about the future of our planet.

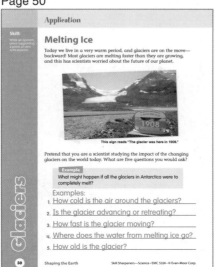

1908

This sign reads "The glacier was here in 1908."

Pretend that you are a scientist studying the impact of the changing glaciers on the world today. What are five questions you would ask?

Example
What might happen if all the glaciers in Antarctica were to completely melt?

Examples:

1. How cold is the air around the glaciers?

2. Is the glacier advancing or retreating?

3. How fast is the glacier moving?

4. Where does the water from melting ice go?

5. How old is the glacier?

Glaciers

50   Shaping the Earth   Skill Sharpeners—Science • EMC 5324 • © Evan-Moor Corp.

Reading

A Surface Made of Plates

Define It!

fault: a break in Earth's crust where blocks of rock are moving in different directions

gradual: taking place slowly

mantle: a layer of molten rock beneath Earth's crust

plates: large sections of Earth's crust

The outer layer of Earth is called the crust. The crust is made of different kinds of rock. Earth's crust is broken into many large pieces called **plates**. All the land and oceans on Earth lie on top of these plates. Beneath the plates is the hot, soft **mantle**. The mantle moves and carries the plates along with it.

The movement of plates can be **gradual** or sudden. When plates move suddenly, an earthquake happens. Part of the ground may lift up several feet, or cracks in the earth may appear. The place where Earth's crust breaks is called a **fault**.

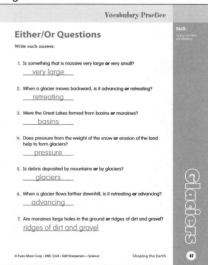

Use the map to find where you live. Write the name of the plate you are on.

Answers will vary.

Concepts: Earth's crust is made up of plates. When the plates move suddenly, an earthquake happens.

Earthquakes

© Evan-Moor Corp. • EMC 5324 • Skill Sharpeners—Science   Shaping the Earth   51

Page 52

Concepts:
Earthquakes happen along the boundaries of plates.

Plates interact along their boundaries in different ways.

Define It!

boundary: a border or an edge

collide: to crash into; to come together

interact: to act on one another

Moving Plates

Earthquakes happen along the **boundaries** of plates, or where the edge of one plate meets another. Plates **interact** along their boundaries as they move in different directions.

Some plates slide past each other. The famous San Andreas Fault in California is an example of plates sliding in opposite directions. Other plates **collide**, or run into each other. When plates collide, they cause powerful earthquakes and can even build mountains. The Himalaya Mountains in Asia are the result of two plates colliding. In other places, plates move apart from each other. This does not cause very strong earthquakes, but ocean basins are often created when two plates pull apart.

Write whether the diagrams above show plates *sliding past* each other, *colliding*, or *moving apart*.

1. <u>moving apart</u>   3. <u>colliding</u>
2. <u>sliding past</u>

Earthquakes

52 | Shaping the Earth | Skill Sharpeners—Science • EMC 5324 • © Evan-Moor Corp.

Page 53

Measuring Earthquakes

Define It!

duration: the length of time that something lasts

magnitude: a measure of the amount of energy released by an earthquake

seismometer: a tool that records movements in Earth's crust

Scientists study earthquakes with a tool called a **seismometer**, which detects and records movement in the ground. When an earthquake happens, a seismometer will display a series of zigzag lines that allow scientists to figure out the **duration** and strength of the quake.

In 1935, a scientist named Charles Richter invented a system of measuring earthquakes. This is called the Richter scale. An earthquake is given a number from 1 to 10 to describe its **magnitude**. A magnitude 1 earthquake is so weak that you can't feel it. An 8.0 earthquake would knock you off your feet! Since scientists began using the Richter scale, the strongest earthquake ever recorded was a 9.5 in Chile in 1960.

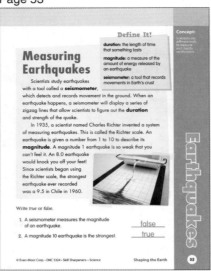

Write *true* or *false*.

1. A seismometer measures the magnitude of an earthquake. — <u>false</u>

2. A magnitude 10 earthquake is the strongest. — <u>true</u>

Concept:
Scientists use different tools to measure and classify earthquakes.

© Evan-Moor Corp. • EMC 5324 • Skill Sharpeners—Science | Shaping the Earth | 53

Page 54

Skill:
Interpret information in graphic representations.

Visual Literacy

Richter Scale

This chart shows the effects of earthquakes of different magnitudes around the world, as well as how many of them are recorded per year. Use the information in the chart to complete the sentences below.

Richter Scale Magnitude	Average Number of Earthquakes (per year)	Earthquake Effects
2.0–2.9	1,300,000	Not felt but are recorded on seismometers
3.0–3.9	130,000	Barely noticeable; hanging objects may swing
4.0–4.9	13,000	Most people notice them; buildings shake
5.0–5.9	1,300	Everyone notices them; windows may break
6.0–6.9	134	Walls may crack; chimneys may fall
7.0–7.9	18	Ground cracks; weak buildings fall down
8.0–8.9	1	Many buildings fall; bridges collapse
9.0–9.9	1 per 20 years	Complete devastation over a wide area
10.0+	Extremely rare	Never recorded

1. Earthquakes of a magnitude of 9.0 happen at a rate of about <u>1</u> every <u>20</u> years.

2. Usually, an earthquake must be at least a magnitude of <u>7.0</u> to cause any buildings to fall down.

3. Most people notice earthquakes that are a magnitude of <u>4.0</u> or greater.

4. The number of earthquakes between magnitudes of 3.0 and 6.9 that happen every year is about <u>144,434</u>

Earthquakes

54 | Shaping the Earth | Skill Sharpeners—Science • EMC 5324 • © Evan-Moor Corp.

Page 55

Vocabulary Practice

Earthquakes Crossword Puzzle

Use the vocabulary words to complete the crossword puzzle.

seismometer	duration	mantle	collide
boundary	interact	plates	fault

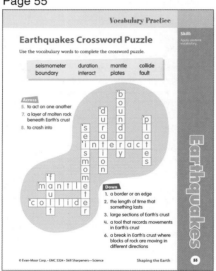

Across

5. to act on one another
7. a layer of molten rock beneath Earth's crust
8. to crash into

Down

1. a border or an edge
2. the length of time that something lasts
3. large sections of Earth's crust
4. a tool that records movements in Earth's crust
6. a break in Earth's crust where blocks of rock are moving in different directions

Skill:
Apply content vocabulary.

Earthquakes

© Evan-Moor Corp. • EMC 5324 • Skill Sharpeners—Science | Shaping the Earth | 55

Page 57

Earthquake-Proof, continued

Directions

1. Prepare the gelatin with an adult the night before the experiment, following the instructions. Pour the gelatin mixture into the baking dish so that it completely covers the bottom of the dish and is at least 1" thick.

2. Put plastic wrap on the baking dish and place it in the refrigerator.

3. The next day, use the marshmallows and toothpicks to create two different buildings: one that you think will stand up to an earthquake, and one that you think will fall down. Place them on top of the gelatin in the baking dish.

4. First, shake the baking dish back and forth slowly and softly. Next, shake it quickly and forcefully. Then answer the questions.

What Did You Discover?

1. What happened when you shook the dish softly? Did either of your buildings fall over? Which one seemed stronger?
   <u>Answers will vary.</u>

2. What happened when you shook the dish harder? Did either of your buildings fall over? Which one seemed stronger?
   <u>Answers will vary.</u>

3. What might you do to make your buildings stronger?
   <u>Answers will vary.</u>

Earthquakes

© Evan-Moor Corp. • EMC 5324 • Skill Sharpeners—Science | Shaping the Earth | 57

Page 58

Skills:
Collect, record, and analyze information.

Application

Famous Earthquakes

There are many places on Earth where earthquakes happen often. Sometimes these earthquakes are so strong that they cause a lot of damage. People remember these earthquakes for years and years. Choose one of the areas below and research to find out about a famous earthquake that happened in that area. Then use the research to answer the questions.

Japan	Alaska	California	Indonesia	Chile

1. Where did the earthquake take place? <u>Answers will vary.</u>

2. When did the earthquake take place? _____

3. What was the magnitude of the earthquake? _____

4. What effect did the earthquake have on the surrounding area? What type of damage did it do? Did it cause any other types of natural disasters (tsunamis, landslides, etc.)?

_____

_____

_____

_____

Earthquakes

58 | Shaping the Earth | Skill Sharpeners—Science • EMC 5324 • © Evan-Moor Corp.

Page 59

Reading

Where Are Volcanoes?

Define It!

active: a volcano that is currently erupting, showing signs of erupting, or has erupted recently

dormant: a volcano that hasn't erupted recently, but is expected to erupt again

erupt: to release lava, ash, and gases

extinct: a volcano that will likely not erupt again

There are thousands of volcanoes on our planet. Most of them are **dormant** or **extinct**. This means that they haven't **erupted** for a long time, or they will not erupt again. However, about 1,500 volcanoes on Earth are still **active**. This means that they have erupted recently and could erupt again in the future.

Most of the world's active volcanoes are in an area called the Ring of Fire. The Ring of Fire is a band of volcanoes that circles the Pacific Ocean. These volcanoes are mostly located along the boundary of the Pacific Plate.

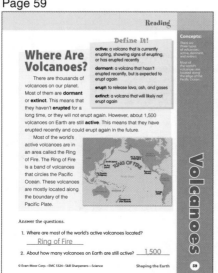

Answer the questions.

1. Where are most of the world's active volcanoes located?
   <u>Ring of Fire</u>

2. About how many volcanoes on Earth are still active? <u>1,500</u>

Concepts:
There are three types of volcanoes: active, dormant, and extinct.

Most of the world's volcanoes are located along the edge of the Pacific Ocean.

Volcanoes

© Evan-Moor Corp. • EMC 5324 • Skill Sharpeners—Science | Shaping the Earth | 59

Page 60

Concepts:
Hot molten rock within Earth's crust is called magma.

Hot molten rock that erupts from a volcano is called lava.

From Magma to Lava

Define It!

lava: hot melted rock that flows from a volcano

magma: hot melted rock that comes from Earth's mantle

vent: an opening in a volcano through which lava can flow

We may see volcanoes rise high above Earth's surface, but they also reach down into the middle layer of Earth, the mantle. Volcanoes form when hot rock rises from the mantle through cracks in the crust. The hot, soft rock of the mantle is always moving. As the rock gets closer to the crust, there is less pressure pushing against it. The rock begins to expand and turns from a solid into liquid **magma**.

When a volcano erupts, magma pushes up through a tube in the volcano and out of its **vent**. When magma reaches the surface, we call it **lava**. As lava cools, it turns from a liquid back into a solid. Now it is a hard rock, not soft the way it was in the mantle.

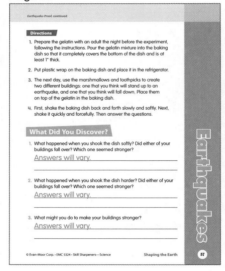

Composite Volcano

Write *true* or *false*.

1. Magma comes from the mantle. — <u>true</u>

2. As magma cools on Earth's surface, it becomes hard rock. — <u>false</u>

Volcanoes

60 | Shaping the Earth | Skill Sharpeners—Science • EMC 5324 • © Evan-Moor Corp.

Page 61

Ways Volcanoes Erupt

Define It!

chamber: a space inside something

debris: small pieces of broken rock, lava, and other materials blown out during an eruption

violent: very strong or powerful

When volcanoes erupt, they can be either **violent** or quiet and steady. Quiet, steady eruptions are known as lava flows. Lava pours through a vent in the crust onto Earth's surface in a slow, constant stream. The Hawaiian Islands were created by this kind of eruption.

Violent eruptions mostly happen in volcanoes that have a deep **chamber** that fills with magma. As magma fills the chamber, it releases gases. These gases build up under the layers of rock at the top of the volcano. Eventually, the pressure is so great that the volcano explodes, sending ash, gases, and other materials blown out during an eruption **debris** into the air. The eruption that destroyed the ancient city of Pompeii in Italy is an example of a violent eruption.

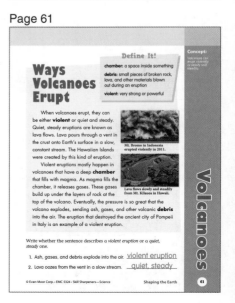

Mt. Bromo in Indonesia erupted violently in 2011.

Lava flows slowly and steadily from Mt. Kilauea in Hawaii.

Write whether the sentence describes a *violent eruption* or a *quiet, steady eruption*.

1. Ash, gases, and debris explode into the air. <u>violent eruption</u>

2. Lava oozes from the vent in a slow stream. <u>quiet, steady</u>

Concept:
Volcanoes can erupt violently or slowly and steadily.

Volcanoes

© Evan-Moor Corp. • EMC 5324 • Skill Sharpeners—Science | Shaping the Earth | 61

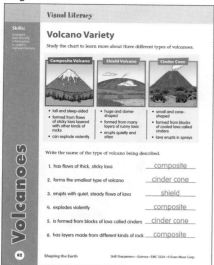

Visual Literacy

Skills:
Interpret and identify information in graphic representations

Volcano Variety

Study the chart to learn more about three different types of volcanoes.

Composite Volcano	Shield Volcano	Cinder Cone
• tall and steep-sided	• huge and dome-shaped	• small and cone-shaped
• formed from flows of sticky lava layered with other kinds of rocks	• formed from many layers of runny lava	• formed from blocks of cooled lava called cinders
• can explode violently	• erupts quietly and often	• lava erupts in sprays

Write the name of the type of volcano being described.

1. has flows of thick, sticky lava — composite
2. forms the smallest type of volcano — cinder cone
3. erupts with quiet, steady flows of lava — shield
4. explodes violently — composite
5. is formed from blocks of lava called cinders — cinder cone
6. has layers made from different kinds of rock — composite

Volcanoes

62   Shaping the Earth   Skill Sharpeners—Science • EMC 5324 • © Evan-Moor Corp.

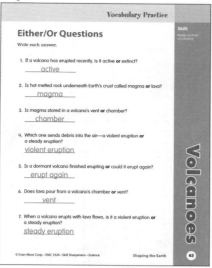

Vocabulary Practice

Skill: Apply content vocabulary

Either/Or Questions

Write each answer.

1. If a volcano has erupted recently, is it active **or** extinct?
   active

2. Is hot melted rock underneath Earth's crust called magma **or** lava?
   magma

3. Is magma stored in a volcano's vent **or** chamber?
   chamber

4. Which one sends debris into the air—a violent eruption **or** a steady eruption?
   violent eruption

5. Is a dormant volcano finished erupting **or** could it erupt again?
   erupt again

6. Does lava pour from a volcano's chamber **or** vent?
   vent

7. When a volcano erupts with lava flows, is it a violent eruption **or** a steady eruption?
   steady eruption

Volcanoes

© Evan-Moor Corp. • EMC 5324 • Skill Sharpeners—Science   Shaping the Earth   63

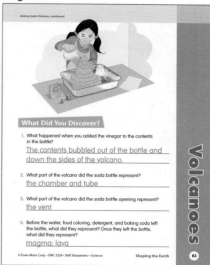

Baking Soda Volcano, continued

What Did You Discover?

1. What happened when you added the vinegar to the contents in the bottle?
   The contents bubbled out of the bottle and down the sides of the volcano.

2. What part of the volcano did the soda bottle represent?
   the chamber and tube

3. What part of the volcano did the soda bottle opening represent?
   the vent

4. Before the water, food coloring, detergent, and baking soda left the bottle, what did they represent? Once they left the bottle, what did they represent?
   magma; lava

Volcanoes

© Evan-Moor Corp. • EMC 5324 • Skill Sharpeners—Science   Shaping the Earth   65

Application

Skill: Write narratives to develop real or imagined experiences or events.

Volcano Alert!

Pretend that you live in a town near an active volcano. One morning, you wake up and see smoke coming out of the volcano's vent! Write a story about what happens next. Be sure to describe the type of volcano you live by. Use what you know about how different types of volcanoes erupt to tell your story.

Answers will vary but should demonstrate an understanding of one type of volcano and how it erupts.

Volcanoes

66   Shaping the Earth   Skill Sharpeners—Science • EMC 5324 • © Evan-Moor Corp.

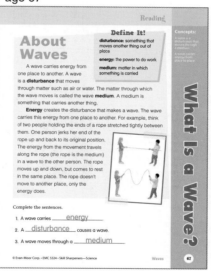

Reading

About Waves

A wave carries energy from one place to another. A wave is a **disturbance** that moves through matter such as air or water. The matter through which the wave moves is called the wave **medium**. A medium is something that carries another thing.

Energy creates the disturbance that makes a wave. The wave carries this energy from one place to another. For example, think of two people holding the ends of a rope stretched tightly between them. One person jerks her end of the rope up and back to its original position. The energy from the movement travels along the rope (the rope is the medium) in a wave to the other person. The rope moves up and down, but comes to rest in the same place. The rope doesn't move to another place, only the energy does.

Define It!

disturbance: something that moves another thing out of place

energy: the power to do work

medium: matter in which something is carried

Concepts:
A wave is a disturbance that moves through a medium.

A wave carries energy from place to place.

Complete the sentences.

1. A wave carries energy
2. A disturbance causes a wave.
3. A wave moves through a medium

What Is a Wave?

© Evan-Moor Corp. • EMC 5324 • Skill Sharpeners—Science   Waves   67

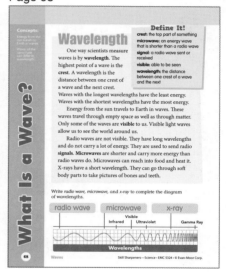

Concepts:
Energy from the sun travels to Earth in waves.

Waves of the same type can differ in wavelength.

Wavelength

One way scientists measure waves is by **wavelength**. The highest point of a wave is the **crest**. A wavelength is the distance between one crest of a wave and the next crest. Waves with the longest wavelengths have the least energy. Waves with the shortest wavelengths have the most energy.

Energy from the sun travels to Earth in waves. These waves travel through empty space as well as through matter. Only some of the waves are **visible** to us. Visible light waves allow us to see the world around us.

Radio waves are not visible. They have long wavelengths and do not carry a lot of energy. They are used to send radio **signals**. **Microwaves** are shorter and carry more energy than radio waves do. Microwaves can reach into food and heat it. **X-rays** have a short wavelength. They can go through soft body parts to take pictures of bones and teeth.

Define It!

crest: the top part of something

microwave: an energy wave that is shorter than a radio wave

signal: a radio wave sent or received

visible: able to be seen

wavelength: the distance between one crest of a wave and the next

Write *radio wave*, *microwave*, and *x-ray* to complete the diagram of wavelengths.

| radio wave | microwave | x-ray |

What Is a Wave?

68   Waves   Skill Sharpeners—Science • EMC 5324 • © Evan-Moor Corp.

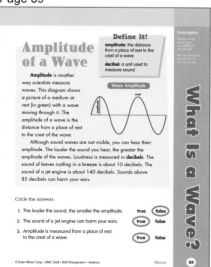

Define It!

amplitude: the distance from a place of rest to the crest of a wave

decibel: a unit used to measure sound

Concepts:
Waves of the same type can differ in amplitude.

We can hear the amplitude of sound waves.

Amplitude of a Wave

Amplitude is another way scientists measure waves. This diagram shows a picture of a medium at rest (in green) with a wave moving through it. The amplitude of a wave is the distance from a place of rest to the crest of the wave.

Although sound waves are not visible, you can hear their amplitude. The louder the sound you hear, the greater the amplitude of the waves. Loudness is measured in **decibels**. The sound of leaves rustling in a breeze is about 10 decibels. The sound of a jet engine is about 140 decibels. Sounds above 85 decibels can harm your ears.

Circle the answers.

1. The louder the sound, the smaller the amplitude.   true   (false)
2. The sound of a jet engine can harm your ears.   (true)   false
3. Amplitude is measured from a place of rest to the crest of a wave.   (true)   false

What Is a Wave?

© Evan-Moor Corp. • EMC 5324 • Skill Sharpeners—Science   Waves   69

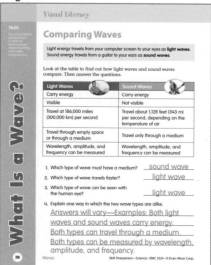

Visual Literacy

Skill: Use information carried from a table to demonstrate understanding and make comparisons.

Comparing Waves

Light energy travels from your computer screen to your eyes as **light waves**. Sound energy travels from a guitar to your ears as **sound waves**.

Look at the table to find out how light waves and sound waves compare. Then answer the questions.

Light Waves	Sound Waves
Carry energy	Carry energy
Visible	Not visible
Travel at 186,000 miles (300,000 km) per second	Travel about 1,128 feet (343 m) per second, depending on the temperature of air
Travel through empty space or through a medium	Travel only through a medium
Wavelength, amplitude, and frequency can be measured	Wavelength, amplitude, and frequency can be measured

1. Which type of wave must have a medium? — sound wave
2. Which type of wave travels faster? — light wave
3. Which type of wave can be seen with the human eye? — light wave
4. Explain one way in which the two wave types are alike.
   Answers will vary—Examples: Both light waves and sound waves carry energy. Both types can travel through a medium. Both types can be measured by wavelength, amplitude, and frequency.

What Is a Wave?

70   Waves   Skill Sharpeners—Science • EMC 5324 • © Evan-Moor Corp.

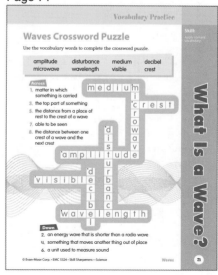

Vocabulary Practice

Skill: Apply content vocabulary

Waves Crossword Puzzle

Use the vocabulary words to complete the crossword puzzle.

| amplitude | disturbance | medium | decibel |
| microwave | wavelength | visible | crest |

Across
1. matter in which something is carried
3. the top part of something
5. the distance from a place of rest to the crest of a wave
7. able to be seen
8. the distance between one crest of a wave and the next crest

(crossword grid answers: medium, crest, microwave, disturbance, amplitude, visible, decibel, wavelength)

Down
2. an energy wave that is shorter than a radio wave
4. something that moves another thing out of place
6. a unit used to measure sound

What Is a Wave?

© Evan-Moor Corp. • EMC 5324 • Skill Sharpeners—Science   Waves   71

Page 72

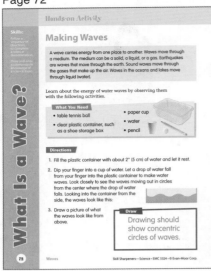

Hands-on Activity

Making Waves

A wave carries energy from one place to another. Waves move through a medium. The medium can be a solid, a liquid, or a gas. Earthquakes are waves that move through the earth. Sound waves move through the gases that make up the air. Waves in the oceans and lakes move through liquid (water).

Learn about the energy of water waves by observing them with the following activities.

What You Need
- table tennis ball
- clear plastic container, such as a shoe storage box
- paper cup
- water
- pencil

Directions

1. Fill the plastic container with about 2" (5 cm) of water and let it rest.

2. Dip your finger into a cup of water. Let a drop of water fall from your finger into the plastic container to make water waves. Look closely to see the waves moving out in circles from the center where the drop of water falls. Looking into the container from the side, the waves look like this:

3. Draw a picture of what the waves look like from above.

Draw
Drawing should show concentric circles of waves.

Skills: **What Is a Wave?**

Page 73

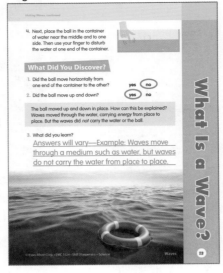

Making Waves, continued

4. Next, place the ball in the container of water near the middle and to one side. Then use your finger to disturb the water at one end of the container.

What Did You Discover?

1. Did the ball move horizontally from one end of the container to the other?   yes (no)

2. Did the ball move up and down?   yes no

The ball moved up and down in place. How can this be explained? Waves moved through the water, carrying *energy* from place to place. But the waves did *not* carry the water or the ball.

3. What did you learn?
Answers will vary—Example: Waves move through a medium such as water, but waves do not carry the water from place to place.

What Is a Wave?

Page 75

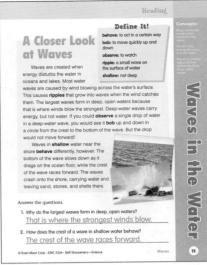

Reading

A Closer Look at Waves

Waves are created when energy disturbs the water in oceans and lakes. Most water waves are caused by wind blowing across the water's surface. This causes **ripples** that grow into waves when the wind catches them. The largest waves form in deep, open waters because that is where winds blow the strongest. Deep-water waves carry energy, but not water. If you could **observe** a single drop of water in a deep-water wave, you would see it **bob** up and down in a circle from the crest to the bottom of the wave. But the drop would not move forward!

Waves in **shallow** water near the shore **behave** differently, however. The bottom of the wave slows down as it drags on the ocean floor, while the crest of the wave races forward. The waves crash onto the shore, carrying water and leaving sand, stones, and shells there.

Define It!
behave: to act in a certain way
bob: to move quickly up and down
observe: to watch
ripple: a small wave on the surface of water
shallow: not deep

Answer the questions.

1. Why do the largest waves form in deep, open waters?
That is where the strongest winds blow.

2. How does the crest of a wave in shallow water behave?
The crest of the wave races forward.

Waves in the Water

Page 76

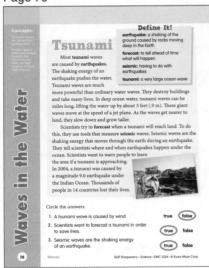

Concepts:

Tsunami

Most **tsunami** waves are caused by **earthquakes**. The shaking energy of an earthquake pushes the water. Tsunami waves are much more powerful than ordinary water waves. They destroy buildings and take many lives. In deep ocean water, tsunami waves can be miles long, lifting the water up by about 3 feet (.9 m). These giant waves move at the speed of a jet plane. As the waves get nearer to land, they slow down and grow taller.

Scientists try to **forecast** when a tsunami will reach land. To do this, they use tools that measure **seismic** waves. Seismic waves are the shaking energy that moves through the earth during an earthquake. They tell scientists where and when earthquakes happen under the ocean. Scientists want to warn people to leave the area if a tsunami is approaching. In 2004, a tsunami was caused by a magnitude 9.0 earthquake under the Indian Ocean. Thousands of people in 14 countries lost their lives.

Define It!
earthquake: a shaking of the ground caused by rocks moving deep in the Earth
forecast: to tell ahead of time what will happen
seismic: having to do with earthquakes
tsunami: a very large ocean wave

Circle the answers.

1. A tsunami wave is caused by wind.   true (false)

2. Scientists want to forecast a tsunami in order to save lives.   (true) false

3. Seismic waves are the shaking energy of an earthquake.   (true) false

Waves in the Water

Page 77

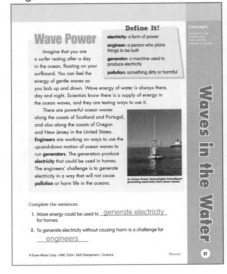

Concept:

Wave Power

Imagine that you are a surfer resting after a day in the ocean, floating on your surfboard. You can feel the energy of gentle waves as you bob up and down. Wave energy of water is always there, day and night. Scientists know there is a supply of energy in the ocean waves, and they are testing ways to use it.

There are powerful ocean waves along the coasts of Scotland and Portugal, and also along the coasts of Oregon and New Jersey in the United States. **Engineers** are working on ways to use the up-and-down motion of ocean waves to run **generators**. The generators produce **electricity** that could be used in homes. The engineers' challenge is to generate electricity in a way that will not cause **pollution** or harm life in the oceans.

Define It!
electricity: a form of power
engineer: a person who plans things to be built
generator: a machine used to produce electricity
pollution: something dirty or harmful

An Ocean Power Technologies PowerBuoy® generating electricity from ocean waves.

Complete the sentences.

1. Wave energy could be used to generate electricity for homes.

2. To generate electricity without causing harm is a challenge for engineers.

Waves in the Water

Page 78

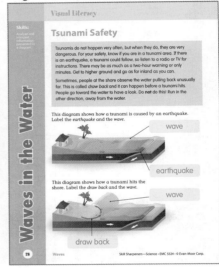

Visual Literacy

Tsunami Safety

Tsunamis do not happen very often, but when they do, they are very dangerous. For your safety, know if you are in a tsunami area. If there is an earthquake, a tsunami could follow, so listen to a radio or TV for instructions. There may be as much as a two-hour warning or only minutes. Get to higher ground and go as far inland as you can.

Sometimes, people at the shore observe the water pulling back unusually far. This is called *draw back* and it can happen before a tsunami hits. People go toward the water to have a look. Do *not* do this! Run in the other direction, away from the water.

This diagram shows how a tsunami is caused by an earthquake. Label the *earthquake* and the *wave*.

wave
earthquake

This diagram shows how a tsunami hits the shore. Label the *draw back* and the *wave*.

wave
draw back

Waves in the Water

Page 79

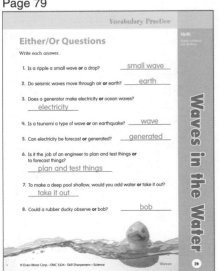

Vocabulary Practice

Either/Or Questions

Write each answer.

1. Is a ripple a small wave **or** a drop?   small wave

2. Do seismic waves move through air **or** earth?   earth

3. Does a generator make electricity **or** ocean waves?
electricity

4. Is a tsunami a type of wave **or** an earthquake?   wave

5. Can electricity be forecast **or** generated?   generated

6. Is it the job of an engineer to plan and test things **or** to forecast things?
plan and test things

7. To make a deep pool shallow, would you add water **or** take it out?
take it out

8. Could a rubber ducky observe **or** bob?   bob

Skill:

Waves in the Water

Page 81

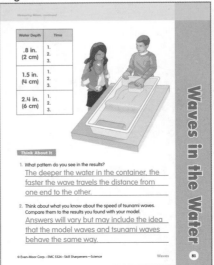

Measuring Waves, continued

Water Depth	Time
.8 in. (2 cm)	1. 2. 3.
1.5 in. (4 cm)	1. 2. 3.
2.4 in. (6 cm)	1. 2. 3.

Think About It

1. What pattern do you see in the results?
The deeper the water in the container, the faster the wave travels the distance from one end to the other.

2. Think about what you know about the speed of tsunami waves. Compare them to the results you found with your model.
Answers will vary but may include the idea that the model waves and tsunami waves behave the same way.

Waves in the Water

Page 82

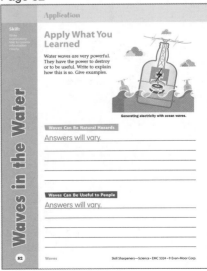

Application

Apply What You Learned

Water waves are very powerful. They have the power to destroy or to be useful. Write to explain how this is so. Give examples.

Generating electricity with ocean waves.

Waves Can Be Natural Hazards
Answers will vary.

Waves Can Be Useful to People
Answers will vary.

Skill:

Waves in the Water

Page 83

Making Sound Waves

Define It!

compress: to squeeze or press

compression: an area where air is squeezed together

particle: a very small piece or speck

rarefaction: an area where air is not closely packed together

vibration: a quick back-and-forth motion

Sound waves are created when an object vibrates, or shakes. The **vibrations** move outward from the object. Sound waves can only move through a medium. They cannot exist in empty space. Most of the sounds we hear travel through air. However, sound waves can also travel through solids, liquids, and gases.

Think of a stretched rubber band. When it is plucked, it vibrates back and forth. As the rubber band moves, it pushes against the air and causes the air **particles** to **compress**, or squeeze together. **Compressions** are areas where air particles are squeezed together. At the edges of the compressions are areas called **rarefactions** where the air particles are not as closely packed together. As more rarefactions and compressions form, they bump into more air and form more waves. When the waves strike our ears, we hear sounds.

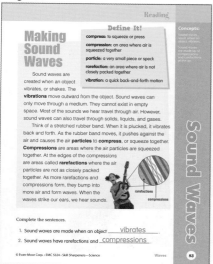

rarefactions
compressions

Complete the sentences.

1. Sound waves are made when an object _vibrates_.

2. Sound waves have rarefactions and _compressions_.

Page 84

Concepts:

Define It!

frequency: the number of waves that pass a certain point, usually in one second

hertz: a measure of frequency

musician: a person who has skill with music

pitch: the highness or lowness of a musical sound

Frequency and Pitch

Sound waves are measured by their **frequency**. The frequency of a wave is the number of waves that pass a certain point, usually in one second. The faster an object vibrates, the greater its frequency. Frequency is measured in **hertz**. One hertz equals one wave per second.

Frequency and **pitch** go together. Pitch is the highness or lowness of a sound. A high-pitched sound, such as a whistle, has a higher frequency than a low-pitched sound, such as a big, deep drum.

Scientists talk about frequency, and **musicians** talk about pitch. A piano has 88 keys that play sounds from low-pitched to high-pitched. The lowest pitch is 28 hertz and the highest pitch is 4,186 hertz.

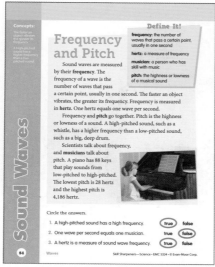

Circle the answers.

1. A high-pitched sound has a high frequency. **(true)** false

2. One wave per second equals one musician. true **(false)**

3. A hertz is a measure of sound wave frequency. **(true)** false

---

Page 85

Define It!

acoustics: the study of sound

affect: to make a change in

architect: a person who plans buildings

decibel: a unit used to measure the loudness of sound

detect: to discover something

Acoustics

Sounds **affect** our lives in many ways every day. **Acoustics** is the study of sound. People may make acoustics their life's work if they are interested in how sound affects us. For example, some scientists study how to make the world quieter for people by making machines less noisy. Other scientists teach the dangers of loud sounds to people's hearing. Acoustical **architects** plan buildings that have safe **decibel** levels for people. Some scientists study how human-made sounds affect how ocean animals behave. Or they may use sound waves to locate and study fish. Some engineers create tools that use sound waves to help doctors **detect** or treat illnesses.

Answer the questions.

1. List two things that can be made with quieter sound levels for people.
machines, buildings

2. How can an architect help save people's hearing?
by planning buildings that have safe decibel levels

Page 86

Safe Listening

The loudness of a sound is measured in decibels. Safe sound levels are below 85 decibels. Any noise at or above 85 decibels can harm our hearing over time. How can you protect your hearing from unsafe noise?

1. Turn down the sound.
2. Walk away from the sound.
3. Block the noise with earplugs or earmuffs.

Read the chart to discover the decibel levels of some common noises.

Is It Too Loud?

140–145	firecracker, jet taking off
130	stock car race
125	balloon popping
115	rock band, ambulance siren
110	car horn, baby crying
105	personal music player
100	snowmobile
90	power mower, food mixer
85	busy city traffic, school lunchroom
60–65	hair dryer
70	dishwasher
60	normal talking
20	whisper

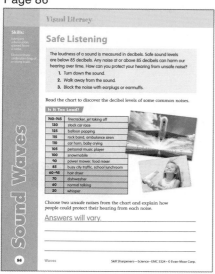

Choose two unsafe noises from the chart and explain how people could protect their hearing from each noise.

Answers will vary.

Page 87

Sound Waves Crossword Puzzle

Use the vocabulary words to complete the crossword puzzle.

frequency	rarefaction	architect	musician
compression	acoustics	vibration	pitch

Across

2. the study of sound
7. the highness or lowness of a musical sound
8. an area where air is not closely packed together

Down

1. an area where air is squeezed together
3. a person who has skill with music
4. a person who plans buildings
5. a quick back-and-forth motion
6. the number of sound waves that pass a given point in a given time

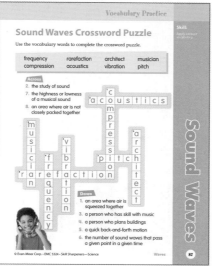

Page 89

Changing Pitch, continued

What Did You Discover?

1. What did you hear? _sound_

2. What did you see? _The rubber band vibrated._

3. Press the rubber band to the ruler at the 2-cm mark and pluck it again. Repeat this at 4, 6, 8, and 10 cm on the ruler. How did the sound change when you pressed down on the rubber band?
The pitch got higher each time.

4. By pressing down on the rubber band, you made the part that was able to vibrate shorter. The shorter the band, the faster it vibrated. What happened to the sound as the rubber band vibrated faster?
The pitch got higher.

5. Predict what will happen to the sound if you start at 10 cm and go backward to 8, 6, 4, and 2 cm.
The pitch will get lower each time.

Complete the sentences. Use the words *higher, lower, faster,* and *slower.*

As the part of the rubber band that can vibrate becomes shorter, the vibrations become _faster_. Faster vibrations make the pitch _higher_.

As the vibrating part of the rubber band becomes longer, the vibrations become _slower_. Slower vibrations make the pitch _lower_.

Page 90

Apply What You Learned

You might be surprised if you counted the number of sounds you hear in a day or even an hour. Make a list of the sounds you hear in the next 10 minutes. Using what you have learned, put the box next to each one that you think has a safe decibel level.

Hint

Safe sound levels are below 85 decibels. Normal talking is about 60 decibels. A school lunchroom is about 85 decibels. A personal music player is about 105 decibels.

☐ _Answers will vary._

Page 91

Telephone Basics

Define It!

disconnect: to switch off

microphone: a tool for sending sound waves, using signals

network: a group of things connected to each other

signal: a pulse or beat of energy

switch: a tool for connecting

Before the telephone was invented, people could not speak to each other from a distance. Today we are able to talk to someone next door or a person on the other side of the world.

The basic parts of your home telephone are a **microphone**, a speaker, and a **switch**. The microphone changes the sound waves of your voice into **signals**. The signals are sent out through the wires in your home to **networks** of wires and radio waves that reach around the world. It all happens in an instant. When the person you are calling speaks back to you, your telephone's speaker goes to work. The speaker changes the signals coming from the other person's telephone into sound waves you can hear.

A switch connects your telephone to the wires when you answer your telephone. Then it **disconnects** your telephone from the network when you end your call.

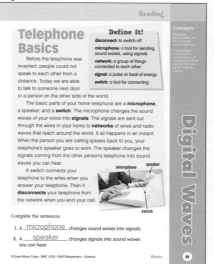

microphone speaker
switch

Complete the sentences.

1. A _microphone_ changes sound waves into signals.

2. A _speaker_ changes signals into sound waves you can hear.

Page 92

Concept:

Define It!

cellular: a type of phone system

honeycomb: something full of small spaces like a beehive

range: the distance able to be reached by radio signals

wireless: using waves instead of wires

Can You Hear Me?

Did you know that a **cellular** telephone, or cellphone, is really a type of radio? Cellphones are **wireless**, unlike many home telephones. When you make a call from a cellphone, signals travel by radio waves to a cellular tower. The cell tower picks up the calls from the radio waves. Most cell towers can pick up signals within 40 miles (64 km) around. This area around a tower is called a cell. The cells of several towers together form a **honeycomb** pattern across a city. When you travel out of **range** of a tower, your phone's signal gets weaker. The cell tower knows this, and sends your signal to a switching office. The switching office sends your call over to the next cell tower. If you ever travel outside the range of the towers, you cannot make a call.

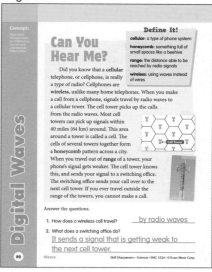

Answer the questions.

1. How does a wireless call travel? _by radio waves_

2. What does a switching office do?
It sends a signal that is getting weak to the next cell tower.

Page 93

Codes and Pixels

The telephone became very popular in the early 1900s. Back then, scientists worked on making a telephone with moving pictures, or **video**. Today, computers send and receive video, too. Computers use a network called the **Internet**.

The Internet is a **digital** network. Speech, writing, and video are changed to a code in order to be sent across the Internet. A digital code uses numerals to send signals. The digital code is sent through a giant network of wire cables and radio waves.

Digital pictures on a TV or a computer screen are made of tiny dots called **pixels**. The pixels are too tiny for you to see each one, but together they form pictures or video.

Define It!
digital: sending signals as a pattern of numerals
Internet: a system of computer networks around the world
pixels: tiny dots of light on a screen that form a picture
video: moving pictures

Circle the answers.
1. The Internet is a computer. true (false)
2. A digital code uses numerals to send signals. (true) false
3. Pixels are tiny dots on a computer screen. (true) false

Digital Waves

Page 94

Stay Connected

Many people have a wireless network at home. A *router* uses radio waves to connect to things in the network. A *modem* connects the network to the Internet. Look at the diagram to find out more.

Read the diagram and answer the questions about it.

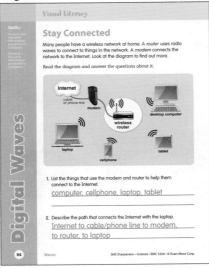

1. List the things that use the modem and router to help them connect to the Internet.
   computer, cellphone, laptop, tablet

2. Describe the path that connects the Internet with the laptop.
   Internet to cable/phone line to modem, to router, to laptop

Digital Waves

Page 95

Either/Or Questions

Write each answer.

1. Are digital pictures made with a microphone or pixels? _pixels_
2. Is a honeycomb a range or a pattern? _pattern_
3. Is the Internet a network or a range? _network_
4. Does a telephone have a pattern or a switch? _switch_
5. Can you hear a sound from a speaker or a pixel? _speaker_
6. Does a digital code use numbers or letters? _numbers_
7. Is a cellular phone soundless or wireless? _wireless_
8. Is video moving air or moving pictures? _moving pictures_

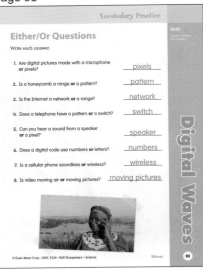

Digital Waves

Page 97

6. Using a pencil, follow the number code to color the picture.

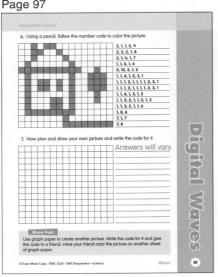

2, 1, 1, 2, 4
2, 2, 2, 1, 8
2, 1, 4, 1, 7
1, 1, 6, 1, 6
0, 10, 2, 1, 2
1, 1, 6, 1, 2, 3, 1
1, 1, 1, 2, 1, 1, 1, 2, 3, 1
1, 1, 6, 1, 3, 1, 2
1, 1, 3, 2, 1, 1, 6
1, 8, 6
7, 1, 7
7, 8

7. Now plan and draw your own picture and write the code for it.
Answers will vary.

More Fun!
Use graph paper to create another picture. Write the code for it and give the code to a friend. Have your friend color the picture on another sheet of graph paper.

Digital Waves

Page 98

Apply What You Learned

Pretend that your family is taking a road trip west. Your dad wants to call your grandmother to tell her you will arrive tomorrow. But his cellphone won't make the call. Use what you know about cellphones, cellular towers, and networks to explain why.

Answers will vary—Example: Cellphones work on radio waves. The signal travels by radio waves from the cellphone to the cellular tower. Cell towers pick up signals within 40 miles around. The family is out of range, so the signal is weak. They are probably more than 40 miles away from the nearest cell tower in the network.

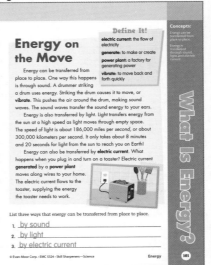

Digital Waves

Page 99

A Law of Energy

Have you ever seen a bolt of lightning flash across the sky? Then you have seen a giant spark of energy. But what is energy? Scientists cannot say exactly what energy is. They do know some things about energy, however. Energy makes it possible to do **work**; that is, to cause something to move. It takes energy for you to run, and it takes energy for a car to move.

Scientists also know that energy can be neither created nor destroyed. This is known as the **law** of **conservation** of energy. If a girl runs across a soccer field and kicks a ball, the energy is **transferred** from the girl's body to the ball. The ball is set in motion. The energy is not lost. Scientists think that the total amount of energy in the entire **universe** always stays the same.

Define It!
conservation: saving the total amount of something
law: something that always happens under the same conditions
transfer: to move from one place to another
universe: all of matter and space
work: the use of force to move an object

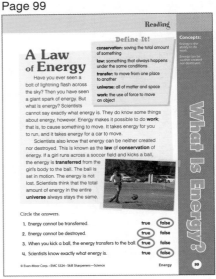

Circle the answers.
1. Energy cannot be transferred. true (false)
2. Energy cannot be destroyed. (true) false
3. When you kick a ball, the energy transfers to the ball. (true) false
4. Scientists know exactly what energy is. true (false)

What Is Energy?

Page 100

Thinking About Energy

Scientists describe energy in two ways. **Potential** energy is stored energy. For example, the food you eat for breakfast gives you energy for your day. Energy from the food is stored up in your body. Your body uses the energy when you run a race or give someone a push on a swing at recess. A bowling ball lifted into the air has potential energy and so does a folded-up toy spring.

Kinetic energy is the energy of motion. An object that is moving from one place to another has kinetic energy. Think of a fast-moving car that **collides** with a road sign, knocking it over. The same car moving at a slow speed only bends the sign when they collide. This is because faster objects have more kinetic energy.

Define It!
collide: to bump into
kinetic: having to do with motion
potential: the stored energy belonging to something

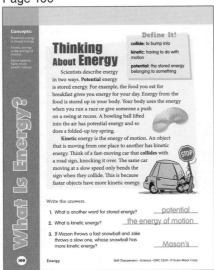

Write the answers.
1. What is another word for stored energy? _potential_
2. What is kinetic energy? _the energy of motion_
3. If Mason throws a fast snowball and Jake throws a slow one, whose snowball has more kinetic energy? _Mason's_

What Is Energy?

Page 101

Energy on the Move

Energy can be transferred from place to place. One way this happens is through sound. A drummer striking a drum uses energy. Striking the drum causes it to move, or **vibrate**. This pushes the air around the drum, making sound waves. The sound waves transfer the sound energy to your ears.

Energy is also transferred by light. Light transfers energy from the sun at a high speed as light moves through empty space. The speed of light is about 186,000 miles per second, or about 300,000 kilometers per second. It only takes about 8 minutes and 20 seconds for light from the sun to reach you on Earth!

Energy can also be transferred by **electric current**. What happens when you plug in and turn on a toaster? Electric current **generated** by a **power plant** moves along wires to your home. The electric current flows to the toaster, supplying the energy the toaster needs to work.

Define It!
electric current: the flow of electricity
generate: to make or create
power plant: a factory for generating power
vibrate: to move back and forth quickly

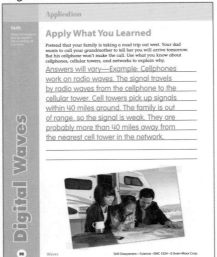

List three ways that energy can be transferred from place to place.
1. _by sound_
2. _by light_
3. _by electric current_

What Is Energy?

Page 102

We Use Energy

Think of the many things in a home that use some form of energy to make them work. *Appliances* such as refrigerators, washers, dryers, and dishwashers use energy. *Electronics* such as computers and televisions use it. Heating systems, air conditioners, and lights all use energy. This graph shows how energy is used in homes.

Read the graph and answer the questions.

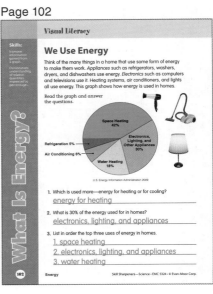

Space Heating 42%
Electronics, Lighting, and Other Appliances 30%
Water Heating 18%
Air Conditioning 6%
Refrigeration 5%

U.S. Energy Information Administration 2009

1. Which is used more—energy for heating or for cooling?
   energy for heating
2. What is 30% of the energy used for in homes?
   electronics, lighting, and appliances
3. List in order the top three uses of energy in homes.
   1. space heating
   2. electronics, lighting, and appliances
   3. water heating

What Is Energy?

Page 103

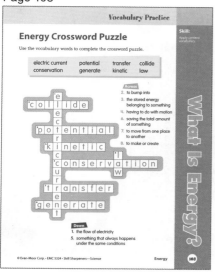

Vocabulary Practice

Energy Crossword Puzzle

Use the vocabulary words to complete the crossword puzzle.

| electric current | potential | transfer | collide |
| conservation | generate | kinetic | law |

Across
2. to bump into
3. the stored energy belonging to something
4. having to do with motion
6. saving the total amount of something
7. to move from one place to another
8. to make or create

Across answers:
- collide
- potential
- kinetic
- conservation
- transfer
- generate

Down
1. the flow of electricity
5. something that always happens under the same conditions

What Is Energy?

Page 104

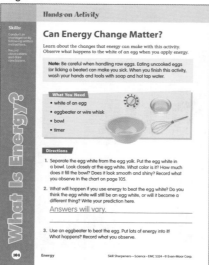

Hands-on Activity

Can Energy Change Matter?

Learn about the changes that energy can make with this activity. Observe what happens to the white of an egg when you apply energy.

Note: Be careful when handling raw eggs (or licking a beater) can make you sick. When you finish this activity, wash your hands and tools with soap and hot tap water.

What You Need
- white of an egg
- eggbeater or wire whisk
- bowl
- timer

Directions
1. Separate the egg white from the egg yolk. Put the egg white in a bowl. Look closely at the egg white. What color is it? How much does it fill the bowl? Does it look smooth and shiny? Record what you observe in the chart on page 105.
2. What will happen if you use energy to beat the egg white? Do you think the egg white will still be an egg white, or will it become a different thing? Write your prediction here.

Answers will vary.

3. Use an eggbeater to beat the egg. Put lots of energy into it! What happens? Record what you observe.

What Is Energy?

Page 105

Can Energy Change Matter?, continued

Time	Appearance of Egg White
Before beating	
After beating	
5 minutes later	
10 minutes later	
15 minutes later	
20 minutes later	
25 minutes later	

4. Do you think it is still an egg white after beating, or has it become a different thing? Give your reasons.

It is still an egg white. Energy changed the way it looks.

5. Let the egg white stand for 5 minutes. Then record what you observe in the chart. Do the same thing after 10, 15, 20, and 25 minutes.
6. Do you think that the matter that is left in the bowl after 25 minutes is the same matter you started with? Why?

Yes, because energy only changed the look of the egg white.

Did You Know?
A *physical change* is any change in matter that does not produce new matter. You observed that the energy of beating the egg white changed the look of it, but it was still an egg white. If you repeat the steps, it will still be an egg white. The energy causes a physical change.

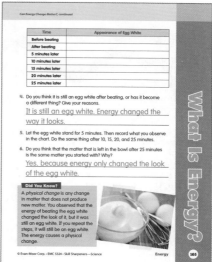

What Is Energy?

Page 106

Application

Apply What You Learned

Look closely at the two pictures. Describe what is happening in each picture. Then explain what type of energy is shown.

Hint
Potential energy is stored energy.
Kinetic energy is energy in motion.

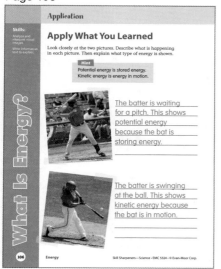

The batter is waiting for a pitch. This shows potential energy because the bat is storing energy.

The batter is swinging at the ball. This shows kinetic energy because the bat is in motion.

What Is Energy?

Page 107

Reading

Heat on the Move

Define It!
molecule: the smallest particle of matter
particle: a very small piece or speck
temperature: a measure of how hot or cold something is

Have you ever warmed your hands by the fire? Then you know something about heat energy. Heat from the fire flowed to your cold hands and warmed them up.

Heat energy moves between things that have different **temperatures**. What happens when an ice cube is added to a bowl of hot soup? Coldness from the ice cube does not flow to the soup. The soup cools because heat from the soup flows to the ice cube. Heat energy flows from warm objects to cool ones.

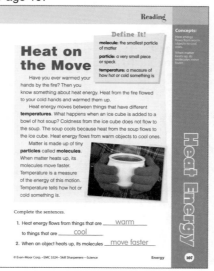

Matter is made up of tiny **particles** called **molecules**. When matter heats up, its molecules move faster. Temperature is a measure of the energy of this motion. Temperature tells how hot or cold something is.

Complete the sentences.
1. Heat energy flows from things that are ___warm___ to things that are ___cool___
2. When an object heats up, its molecules ___move faster___

Heat Energy

Page 108

Concepts:

Molecules in Motion

Define It!
conduction: the transfer of heat when there is a difference in temperatures
conductor: matter that provides an easy path for the flow of heat or other energy
transfer: to move from one place to another

Conduction is one way that heat energy is **transferred**. Conduction happens when two things are touching each other. For example, a metal spoon grows warm in a cup of hot tea. Why does this happen? When molecules bump into each other, heat energy is transferred. The heat moves from the faster-moving molecules of the hot tea to the slower-moving molecules of the cold spoon. The slower-moving molecules gain heat energy and speed up. Heat energy is transferred from one molecule to another until all the molecules in the tea and the spoon are moving at the same speed. The temperature of the tea and the temperature of the metal spoon become the same.

Metal is a good **conductor** because heat energy moves quickly through it. Cooking pots are metal because they quickly transfer heat energy from a stove to the food.

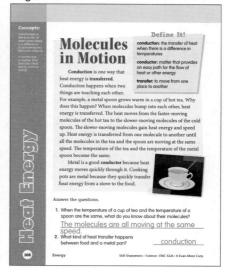

Answer the questions.
1. When the temperature of a cup of tea and the temperature of a spoon are the same, what do you know about their molecules?
The molecules are all moving at the same speed.
2. What kind of heat transfer happens between food and a metal pan? ___conduction___

Heat Energy

Page 109

More About Heat

Define It!
convection: the transfer of heat energy, causing movement in liquids and gases
current: a flow
radiation: the transfer of heat through waves
solar: from the sun

Concepts:

Convection is a second way that heat energy is transferred. Convection happens in liquids and gases, causing convection currents. Think of a pan of water on the stove. When the liquid gains heat energy, its molecules move faster and begin to spread out. When this happens, the heated liquid begins to rise. This causes **currents**, or flow, in the liquid. Currents formed in this way are called convection currents.

Radiation is a third way that heat is transferred. The sun is an example of radiation. The sun and other stars are always giving off energy. **Solar** energy travels to Earth through empty space in waves. Light waves, radio waves, and microwaves are some types of radiation from the sun.

Circle the answers.
1. Molecules of a liquid spread out when they are heated. **true** / false
2. Convection currents may form in liquids and gases. **true** / false
3. Radiation does not transfer heat. true / **false**

Heat Energy

Page 110

Visual Literacy

Heat and Weather

The sun's **radiation** warms the land on Earth. Then heat transfers from the land to the air by **conduction**. The air becomes warmer and lighter, so it rises. **Convection currents** begin to form. As the air goes higher into the sky, it begins to cool. When the air grows cool, it becomes heavier and sinks back toward land. Convection currents can cause breezes, winds, thunderstorms, and even hurricanes.

Label the diagram using the words *radiation*, *conduction*, and *convection currents*.

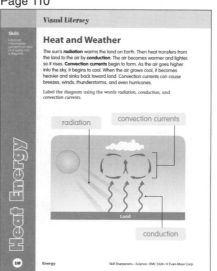

radiation

convection currents

Land

conduction

Heat Energy

Page 111

Vocabulary Practice

Either/Or Questions

Write each answer.

1. Are molecules particles of matter **or** empty space?
   particles of matter
2. Is temperature a measure of how far away something is **or** how cold it is?
   how cold it is
3. Does the sun's energy reach Earth by conduction **or** radiation?
   radiation
4. Do currents cause breezes **or** radio waves? breezes
5. Is metal a conductor **or** a current? conductor
6. Does solar energy come from liquids **or** from the sun?
   the sun
7. Does convection make currents **or** particles? currents
8. Does conduction happen when temperatures are the same **or** when they are different?
   different

Heat Energy

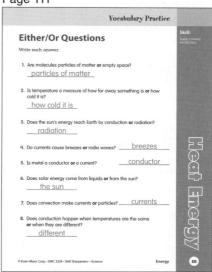

Page 113

Purple Swirl, continued

What Did You Discover?

1. In what direction did the warmer red-colored water move?
   Water moved from the side above the hot cup to the side above the cold cup.

2. Use what you know about the transfer of heat energy to explain why the water did this.
   Heat flowed from the warmer thing to the cooler one.

3. What were the swirls of color that you observed?
   They were convection currents.

4. What happened to the colors when you waited awhile longer?
   The red and blue coloring mixed to make the water purple.

5. What do you think is true about the temperature of all the molecules in the purple water?
   All of the molecules are the same temperature.

Heat Energy

© Evan-Moor Corp. • EMC 5324 • Skill Sharpeners—Science   Energy   113

Page 114

Application

Apply What You Learned

Pretend that you are a molecule of water. One day, you are put into a soup pot on the stove. What happens next? Tell your story.

Hint
Heat energy makes molecules move faster and spread out. Convection currents begin to form when heated liquid rises.

Answers will vary but should be a narrative that includes an understanding of how heat energy makes molecules move faster and spread out, and how convection currents form when heated liquid rises.

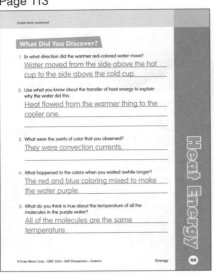

Heat Energy

114   Energy   Skill Sharpeners—Science • EMC 5324 • © Evan-Moor Corp.

Page 115

Reading

Making Electricity

Define It!
generator: a machine that produces electricity
hydroelectricity: electricity made from water power
rotor: part of a machine that turns
shaft: a long rod used in a machine
turbine: a machine with a wheel for making power

Most electricity in the United States is made by power plants that burn natural gas, coal, and oil. But a small amount of the electricity we use comes from wind. Wind **turbines** change the kinetic energy of wind into electrical energy. Wind turns the giant turbine blades. The blades turn a **rotor** that turns a **shaft**. The shaft spins a **generator** that makes electric current. The electric current travels through wires to homes, schools, and other places.

Another small part of the electricity produced comes from the power of moving water. This is called **hydroelectricity**. (*Hydro* means "water.") Water falling over a dam has enough force to spin the blades of giant turbines. The energy of the turbines is changed into electricity.

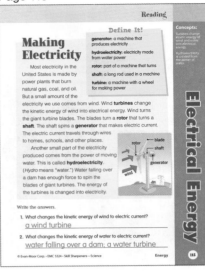

Write the answers.

1. What changes the kinetic energy of wind to electric current?
   a wind turbine

2. What changes the kinetic energy of water to electric current?
   water falling over a dam; a water turbine

Electrical Energy

© Evan-Moor Corp. • EMC 5324 • Skill Sharpeners—Science   Energy   115

Page 116

Concepts:

The Electric Toaster

Define It!
circuit: a closed path or loop through which electricity can flow
filament: a fine wire
lever: a bar used to operate a machine
resistor: something that limits the flow of electric current

An electric toaster is not as simple as it looks. When you push the **lever** down on a toaster, a switch completes a **circuit**. This sends electric current flowing through the toaster. Electric current flowing through a circuit can turn into heat. Inventors had a hard time figuring out how to make a toaster that wouldn't catch fire! They knew that electricity flows through conductors, such as metal. They also knew that some metals were not as good at conducting heat as others. Those metals are called **resistors**.

The glowing, red-hot **filaments** inside a toaster are resistors. The problem was how to keep the filaments from melting or burning. Albert Marsh solved the problem. He created a wire from two metals: nickel and chromium (KROH-me-uhm). The wire was a good resistor and could stand up to very high heat. This type of wire is still used in toasters today.

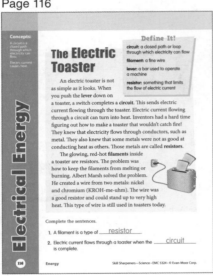

Complete the sentences.

1. A filament is a type of   resistor

2. Electric current flows through a toaster when the   circuit   is complete.

Electrical Energy

116   Energy   Skill Sharpeners—Science • EMC 5324 • © Evan-Moor Corp.

Page 117

Electricity and Light

Define It!
digital: showing time by displaying numerals (digits)
display: information shown on a screen
LED: a type of light used in many devices
segment: one part of something that has been divided

Long ago, people lit fires when night fell. Today we can flip a switch and electricity will travel through a circuit to give us light. An **LED** is one type of light. LEDs are all around us. For example, they form the lighted numbers on **digital** clocks. An LED is a tiny light bulb that fits into an electrical circuit. Each clock number is divided into seven parts, or **segments**. Each segment is an LED that is connected separately to the circuit. When one of the LEDs receives electric current, that segment lights up. The time displayed on the clock changes as segments are turned on and off. For example, when all seven of the LED segments in a number are turned on, the **display** shows the number *8*. The clock has a counter that tells it when to change numbers and display the correct time.

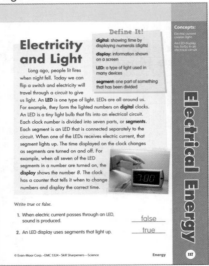

Write *true* or *false*.

1. When electric current passes through an LED, sound is produced.   false

2. An LED display uses segments that light up.   true

Electrical Energy

© Evan-Moor Corp. • EMC 5324 • Skill Sharpeners—Science   Energy   117

Page 118

Visual Literacy

Kinds of Energy

Electric currents can move energy from place to place. Electric currents produce heat energy in a toaster and light energy in an LED. They also produce the energy of motion in a fan and the energy of sound in a microphone.

For each picture, list one or more kinds of energy that are being produced from electric currents. Use the words *heat, light, motion,* and *sound*.

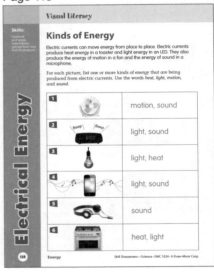

1	motion, sound
2	light, sound
3	light, heat
4	light, sound
5	sound
6	heat, light

Electrical Energy

118   Energy   Skill Sharpeners—Science • EMC 5324 • © Evan-Moor Corp.

Page 119

Vocabulary Practice

Electrical Energy Crossword Puzzle

Use the vocabulary words to complete the crossword puzzle.

hydroelectricity   turbine   display   filament
segment   digital   resistor   circuit

Across
2. a machine for making power with a wheel
3. showing time by displaying numerals
5. a fine wire
6. one part of something that has been divided
7. information shown on a screen
8. a closed path or loop through which electricity can flow

Down
1. electricity made from water power
4. something that limits the flow of electric current

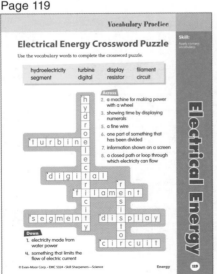

Electrical Energy

© Evan-Moor Corp. • EMC 5324 • Skill Sharpeners—Science   Energy   119

Page 120

Hands-on Activity

An Electromagnet

Electromagnets are used in electric motors. Many of the things you use every day have electromagnets—from doorbells to computers. You can demonstrate that a wire with electric current running through it creates a magnetic field. Make your own electromagnet!

What You Need
- 1.5 volt (AA) battery
- battery holder with clips
- 4 iron nails
- long insulated wire with stripped ends
- paper clips
- tape

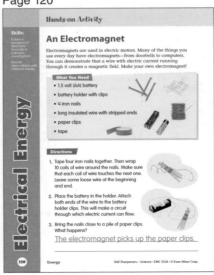

Directions

1. Tape four iron nails together. Then wrap 10 coils of wire around the nails. Make sure that each coil of wire touches the next one. Leave some loose wire at the beginning and end.

2. Place the battery in the holder. Attach both ends of the wire to the battery holder clips. This will make a circuit through which electric current can flow.

3. Bring the nails close to a pile of paper clips. What happens?
   The electromagnet picks up the paper clips.

Electrical Energy

120   Energy   Skill Sharpeners—Science • EMC 5324 • © Evan-Moor Corp.

Page 121

An Electromagnet, continued

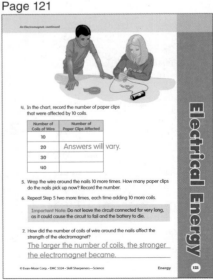

4. In the chart, record the number of paper clips that were affected by 10 coils.

Number of Coils of Wire	Number of Paper Clips Affected
10	
20	Answers will vary.
30	
40	

5. Wrap the wire around the nails 10 more times. How many paper clips do the nails pick up now? Record the number.

6. Repeat Step 5 two more times, each time adding 10 more coils.

Important Note: Do not leave the circuit connected for very long, as it could cause the circuit to fail and the battery to die.

7. How did the number of coils of wire around the nails affect the strength of the electromagnet?
   The larger the number of coils, the stronger the electromagnet became.

Electrical Energy

© Evan-Moor Corp. • EMC 5324 • Skill Sharpeners—Science   Energy   121

Page 122

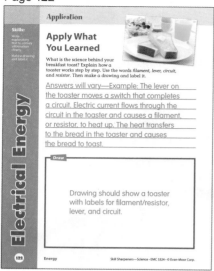

Apply What You Learned

Electrical Energy

What is the science behind your breakfast toast? Explain how a toaster works step by step. Use the words *filament, lever, circuit,* and *resistor.* Then make a drawing and label it.

Answers will vary—Example: The lever on the toaster moves a switch that completes a circuit. Electric current flows through the circuit in the toaster and causes a filament, or resistor, to heat up. The heat transfers to the bread in the toaster and causes the bread to toast.

Draw

Drawing should show a toaster with labels for filament/resistor, lever, and circuit.

Page 123

Reading

Light Travels

Light Energy

The sun and other stars are always giving off energy in the form of **electromagnetic waves**. Light energy from the sun travels at 186,000 miles (300,000 km) per *second* through empty space to reach us on Earth. Other electromagnetic waves such as x-rays, radio waves, and microwaves are **invisible** to us. It is **visible** light that allows us to see the world around us. If you can see an object, that is because light is hitting the object and traveling to your eyes.

People have studied light for hundreds of years, but there is still a lot for scientists to wonder about. Scientists experiment with light to see how it behaves. This can help them to invent new uses for light. For example, a **laser** is a useful tool for doctors that uses a strong beam of light.

Define It!

electromagnetic wave: a wave that travels at the speed of light

invisible: not able to be seen

laser: a tool that uses a strong beam of light

visible: able to be seen

Concepts:
Visible light waves allow us to see the world around us.

Light travels through empty space at 186,000 miles per second.

Answer the questions.

1. What is the only form of electromagnetic waves visible to us?
   visible light
2. What is the speed of light traveling through empty space?
   186,000 miles per second (300,000 km)

Page 124

Concepts:
Light passes through transparent objects.

Translucent objects let some but not all light pass through.

Light cannot pass through opaque objects.

More About Light

Light Energy

Scientists sometimes talk about light as a **ray**, or a thin beam. Light rays move from place to place in a straight line. You see an object when light rays bounce off the object and travel to your eyes. Light rays pass through a **transparent** object, such as a window. **Translucent** objects let *some* light pass through, but not all. For example, sunglasses and tinted car windows are translucent. However, if a light ray hits an **opaque** object, such as a wall, it cannot pass through it. This is how shadows are made. When light can't pass through an object, a shadow is produced on the other side of the object.

Define It!

opaque: not allowing light to pass through

ray: a thin beam of light

translucent: allowing light to pass through, but not all

transparent: allowing light to pass through

Write *true* or *false*.

1. You can see through opaque objects.   false
2. Light moves in a straight line.   true
3. Transparent objects make shadows.   false

Page 125

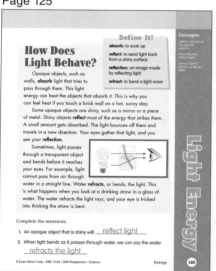

How Does Light Behave?

Light Energy

Opaque objects, such as walls, **absorb** light that tries to pass through them. This light energy can heat the objects that absorb it. This is why you can feel heat if you touch a brick wall on a hot, sunny day.

Some opaque objects are shiny, such as a mirror or a piece of metal. Shiny objects **reflect** most of the energy that strikes them. A small amount gets absorbed. The light bounces off them and travels in a new direction. Your eyes gather that light, and you see your **reflection**.

Sometimes, light passes through a transparent object and bends before it reaches your eyes. For example, light cannot pass from air through water in a straight line. Water **refracts**, or bends, the light. This is what happens when you look at a drinking straw in a glass of water. The water refracts the light rays, and your eye is tricked into thinking the straw is bent.

Define It!

absorb: to soak up

reflect: to send light back from a shiny surface

reflection: an image made by reflecting light

refract: to bend a light wave

Concepts:
Light is absorbed by opaque objects.

Shiny objects reflect light.

Some objects refract, or bend, light.

Complete the sentences.

1. An opaque object that is shiny will ___reflect light___
2. When light bends as it passes through water, we can say the water
   ___refracts the light___

Page 126

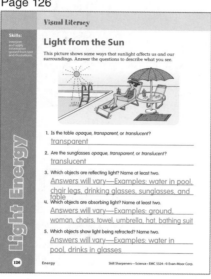

Visual Literacy

Light from the Sun

Light Energy

This picture shows some ways that sunlight affects us and our surroundings. Answer the questions to describe what you see.

1. Is the table *opaque, transparent,* or *translucent?*
   transparent
2. Are the sunglasses *opaque, transparent,* or *translucent?*
   translucent
3. Which objects are reflecting light? Name at least two.
   Answers will vary—Examples: water in pool, chair legs, drinking glasses, sunglasses, and table
4. Which objects are absorbing light? Name at least two.
   Answers will vary—Examples: ground, woman, chairs, towel, umbrella, hat, bathing suit
5. Which objects show light being refracted? Name two.
   Answers will vary—Examples: water in pool, drinks in glasses

---

Page 127

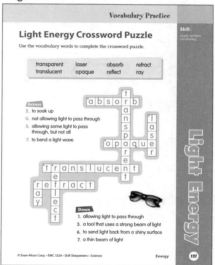

Vocabulary Practice

Light Energy Crossword Puzzle

Light Energy

Use the vocabulary words to complete the crossword puzzle.

| transparent | laser | absorb | refract |
| translucent | opaque | reflect | ray |

Across
2. to soak up
4. not allowing light to pass through
5. allowing some light to pass through, but not all
7. to bend a light wave

Down
1. allowing light to pass through
3. a tool that uses a strong beam of light
6. to send light back from a shiny surface
7. a thin beam of light

Page 129

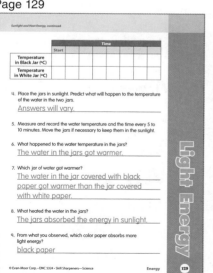

Sunlight and Heat Energy, continued

	Start	Time			
Temperature in Black Jar (ºC)					
Temperature in White Jar (ºC)					

Light Energy

4. Place the jars in sunlight. Predict what will happen to the temperature of the water in the two jars.
   Answers will vary.
5. Measure and record the water temperature and the time every 5 to 10 minutes. Move the jars if necessary to keep them in the sunlight.
6. What happened to the water temperature in the jars?
   The water in the jars got warmer.
7. Which jar of water got warmer?
   The water in the jar covered with black paper got warmer than the jar covered with white paper.
8. What heated the water in the jars?
   The jars absorbed the energy in sunlight.
9. From what you observed, which color paper absorbs more light energy?
   black paper

Page 130

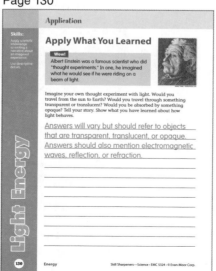

Application

Apply What You Learned

Light Energy

Wow!
Albert Einstein was a famous scientist who did "thought experiments." In one, he imagined what he would see if he were riding on a beam of light.

Imagine your own thought experiment with light. Would you travel from the sun to Earth? Would you travel through something transparent or translucent? Would you be absorbed by something opaque? Tell your story. Show what you have learned about how light behaves.

Answers will vary but should refer to objects that are transparent, translucent, or opaque. Answers should also mention electromagnetic waves, reflection, or refraction.

Here's how parents turn "I'm bored! There's nothing to do!" into "I'm *never* bored!"

The Never-Bored Kid Books

Ages 4–9 This exciting, colorful series will engage kids in hours of productive fun. There are hidden pictures, puzzles, things to cut out and create, pop-ups, art projects, word games, and a whole lot more! **evan-moor.com/nbkb**

The Never-Bored Kid Book

Ages 4–5	EMC 6300
Ages 5–6	EMC 6303
Ages 6–7	EMC 6301
Ages 7–8	EMC 6304
Ages 8–9	EMC 6302

160 full-color pages.

The Never-Bored Kid Book 2

Ages 4–5	EMC 6307
Ages 5–6	EMC 6308
Ages 6–7	EMC 6309
Ages 7–8	EMC 6310
Ages 8–9	EMC 6311

144 full-color pages.

iParenting Media Hot Award Winner

Flashcards

These aren't your average flashcards! Our flashcards include an interactive component with access to online timed tests. The corresponding online activities add another dimension to flashcard practice. Each flashcard set motivates young learners to practice an important readiness concept or fundamental skill.

56 full-color flashcards

56 full-color flashcards.

AGES 4–7+

Reading

Colors and Shapes	Ages 4+	EMC 4161
The Alphabet	Ages 4+	EMC 4162
Vowel Sounds	Ages 5+	EMC 4163
Word Families	Ages 6+	EMC 4164
Sight Words	Ages 6+	EMC 4165

Math

Counting 1–20	Ages 4+	EMC 4166
Counting 1–100	Ages 5+	EMC 4167
Addition and Subtraction Facts to 10	Ages 5+	EMC 4168
Addition Facts 11–18	Ages 6+	EMC 4169
Subtraction Facts 11–18	Ages 6+	EMC 4170
Multiplication Facts to 9s	Ages 7+	EMC 4171
Division Facts to 9s	Ages 7+	EMC 4172

with online timed tests!